LAKE OSWEGO JR. HIGH SCHOOL
2500 SW COUNTRY CLUB RD
LAKE OSWEGO, OR 97034
503-534-2335

Women of Achievement

Barbara Walters

Women *of* Achievement

Abigail Adams
Susan B. Anthony
Tyra Banks
Clara Barton
Hillary Rodham Clinton
Marie Curie
Ellen DeGeneres
Diana, Princess of Wales
Tina Fey
Ruth Bader Ginsburg
Joan of Arc
Helen Keller
Madonna
Michelle Obama
Sandra Day O'Connor
Georgia O'Keeffe
Nancy Pelosi
Rachael Ray
Anita Roddick
Eleanor Roosevelt
Martha Stewart
Barbara Walters
Venus and Serena Williams

Women of Achievement

Barbara Walters

TELEVISION HOST AND PRODUCER

Dennis Abrams

CHELSEA HOUSE
PUBLISHERS
An imprint of Infobase Publishing

Chelsea House
An imprint of Infobase Publishing
132 West 31st Street
New York, NY 10001

Library of Congress Cataloging-in-Publication Data
Abrams, Dennis, 1960-
  Barbara Walters : television host and producer / by Dennis Abrams.
    p. cm. — (Women of achievement)
  Includes bibliographical references and index.
  ISBN 978-1-60413-686-9 (hardcover)
  1. Walters, Barbara, 1931—Juvenile literature. 2. Journalists—United States—Biography—Juvenile literature. 3. Television personalities—United States—Biography—Juvenile literature. I. Title. II. Series.

PN4874.W285A67 2010
070'.92—dc22
[B]
                                        2009052233

Chelsea House books are available at special discounts when purchased in bulk quantities for businesses, associations, institutions, or sales promotions. Please call our Special Sales Department in New York at (212) 967-8800 or (800) 322-8755.

You can find Chelsea House on the World Wide Web at http://www.chelseahouse.com.

Text design by Erik Lindstrom
Cover design by Ben Peterson
Composition by EJB Publishing Services
Cover printed by Bang Printing, Brainerd, Minn.
Book printed and bound by Bang Printing, Brainerd, Minn.
Date printed: August 2010
Printed in the United States of America
10 9 8 7 6 5 4 3 2 1

This book is printed on acid-free paper.

All links and Web addresses were checked and verified to be correct at the time of publication. Because of the dynamic nature of the Web, some addresses and links may have changed since publication and may no longer be valid.

CONTENTS

The Door Opens

For nearly as long as there has been network television, there has been *Today*. It was the brainchild of Pat Weaver, then vice president of the National Broadcasting Company (NBC) and the father of actress Sigourney Weaver. Weaver felt that the time had come for a morning show that would serve as the television version of the morning newspaper, to be broadcast Monday through Friday, live from New York City.

In the very early days of television, the three national television networks—the Columbia Broadcasting System (CBS), the American Broadcasting Company (ABC), and NBC—did not even broadcast shows during daytime hours. Critics at NBC called *Today* "Weaver's Folly." Who, they grumbled, would want to watch television in the morning while they were busily getting ready for work and getting the kids off to school?

It turned out that plenty of people would want to watch. First broadcast on January 14, 1952, *Today* (also referred to as *The Today Show*) set the standard for what morning television could be. Its first host, Dave Garroway, introduced the show by saying:

> Well here we are, and good morning to you. The very first good morning of what I hope and suspect will be a great many good mornings between you and me. Here it is, January 14, 1952, when NBC begins a new program called *Today* and, if it doesn't sound too revolutionary, I really believe this begins a new kind of television.[1]

Indeed, it *was* the first show of its kind on national television, creating an audience ready to watch a morning news television show. The basic format of the show when it premiered in 1952—a blend of news reports, interviews with newsmakers ranging from politicians to movie stars, and lifestyle features and light news items—is the same format that endures today. (There is, however, one major difference in today's version. From 1953 to 1957, *The Today Show* had a mascot, a chimpanzee named J. Fred Muggs who was featured as a kind of humorous sidekick to the show's host, Dave Garroway.)

But while the show had a male host, a male weatherman, and even a male chimpanzee along for the ride, what it did not have was any women in any real position of authority. In the 1950s, a female broadcaster was a rare breed. Reporting the news was largely considered to be "man's business," too serious a task to be assigned to women. Instead, women, with a few notable exceptions such as Nancy Dickerson and Lisa Howard, were relegated to reporting on what were then called "women's stories." The rest of the time, they were made to sit on the sidelines and were told to look pretty and charming and to make the male host look good.

So, while generations of *Today* viewers (since 1952 the show has been, with very few exceptions, the most popular morning show on TV) have grown up watching Jane Pauley, Deborah Norville, Katie Couric, and Meredith Vieira ably fill the position of principal anchor and host of the show, younger viewers may be surprised to learn that it has not always been that way. Even on *The Today Show*, the idea that a woman could possibly be a "real" journalist was not taken seriously for many years.

The lack of respect that women had in journalism in general and on *The Today Show* in particular becomes obvious when looking at the role that they were assigned. Instead of being called a "host" or a "reporter" or an "anchor," they were called the *Today* Girl. Of course, they were not really "girls," they were grown women. But calling them girls only served to illustrate that they were not quite being taken seriously.

Of course, the *Today* Girl was not there to report on the news or to interview world leaders or politicians. Instead, she was there to discuss lighter issues pertaining to fashion and lifestyle. She was also allowed to cover lighter human-interest type stories, maybe interview figures from the world of entertainment, and engage in friendly conversation and banter with the male host—nothing more and nothing less.

As though to emphasize that point, during the first years of *Today*, the role of the *Today* Girl was not given to a serious reporter or journalist, but instead to a series of actresses, including Estelle Parsons, Lee Meriwether, Betsy Palmer, and Florence Henderson, as well as the big-band singer Helen O'Connell. Obviously, during this era, being a journalist was not required to get the job—looking pretty was. Gerry Davis, author of a history of the first 35 years of *The Today Show*, noted:

> The original *Today* was definitely a man's world, although the *Today* Girl was, year by year, to become more prominent and important on the show. The prerequisites for the *Today* Girl were that she be attractive, talented, and witty. Besides that, she had to be feminine, fashion conscious, food wise, family oriented, and, if necessary, able to pour tea.[2]

Perhaps not surprisingly, that attitude regarding the role of women in television was apparent behind the camera as well. In 1961, of *The Today Show*'s eight writers who also had the responsibility of producing interviews and features, only one was a woman. There were never two. That was not a coincidence. Just one female writer was required, since her job, not surprisingly, was to write exclusively for the *Today* Girl. This was the male-dominated world of network television that Barbara Walters entered in 1961.

ENTERING THE FRAY

A graduate of Sarah Lawrence College, Walters had worked in local and national television as both a writer and producer, and she had begun to make a name for herself as a writer before joining *Today*. But when the morning news show she had been working on was canceled and she was unable to find work in television, Walters settled into a career in pubic relations. She was a recent divorcée in her early thirties and working unhappily at *Redbook* magazine when she got a phone call from Fred Freed, the new producer for *The Today Show* who had been her boss on CBS's *The Morning Show* and remembered her work well.

He asked her if she would be interested in returning to television. He could not offer her much: It was a job as a

Barbara Walters appears on NBC's morning program, *Today*, on June 3, 1976, shortly before leaving the network to cohost the evening news on ABC. The ABC deal made her the highest-paid television journalist in the United States.

writer, but only for a limited period of time. *The Today Show* had decided that instead of having a series of commercials from different companies, it would sell a five-minute segment to one company, S&H Green Stamps. Anita Colby, a beautiful ex-model and one-time actress, would be the face of those segments.

It would be Walters's responsibility to create material that would appeal to the female target audience of S&H Green Stamps. The segments that Walters would write for Colby would revolve around such topics as "fashion, trends, beauty tips, how-to advice on such crucial matters as properly tying a scarf, entertaining at home, preparing for the holidays, and so-on."[3] Walters, eager to return to television, jumped at the opportunity. While it did not seem terribly promising, she was determined to make the most of it.

It was a first step in what has been a remarkable professional journey. She quickly went from being a behind-the-scenes writer and producer to an on-air journalist and the first female cohost in the history of *Today*, all before accepting an offer in 1976 that made her the highest-paid television journalist in the United States. And yet, even that was just one stage of her long and illustrious career. As described on the ABC Web site:

> Barbara Walters is a pioneer for women in the news industry. She was the first woman ever to cohost a network news program, served as cohost and chief correspondent for ABC News' *20/20* for 25 years and is both creator and executive producer of *The View*. From Fidel Castro to Miley Cyrus, she has interviewed more statesmen and stars than almost any other journalist in history and *The New York Times* calls her "the interviewer of record."[4]

Yet it has not always been easy. She has been harshly criticized for helping to blur the line between entertainment

IN HER OWN WORDS

Barbara Walters may have worked in different industries, but her career was always in television. Walters once said:

> A job is not a career. I think I started out with a job. It turned into a career and changed my life.

and journalism and was described in the *New Yorker* as being "newsier than other entertainment reporters, and more showbiz than other news reporters."[5] She has been mocked on *Saturday Night Live*. She has struggled, like many other women, to find a balance between having a career and family. And all the while, she has been tirelessly breaking down barriers for female journalists everywhere.

But it was a career that almost did not happen. Greta Van Susteren, interviewing Walters in May 2009 for Fox News, mentioned the fact that female journalists today have a much easier time being taken seriously than Walters did when she was starting out. Walters acknowledged that this was true:

> My path was much tougher. But there is something about being able to do things first that, that, I don't know, that gives you a feeling about yourself, and that gives you a feeling about your career. . . .
>
> When I think of the people that I have met because I have interviewed every president—I was going to say every president since Abraham Lincoln, but that's not true—since Richard Nixon, and almost every world leader, and so on—what a blessed life I have had, and never expected it to happen. It was, in great part, by chance.[6]

How did it happen? How did a shy, insecure Jewish girl from Boston, Massachusetts, go from being a behind-the-scenes writer to the *Today* Girl and the show's eventual cohost? How did she recover from a nearly disastrous move to ABC News to become, in the words of National Association of Broadcasters president Edward O. Fritts, "one of the world's most respected interviewers and journalists . . . [and] one of America's great news personalities"?[7]

For Barbara Walters, like many other successful people, her story begins with family.

Childhood

It may not be altogether surprising that Walters, whose career has long straddled the gap between entertainment and news, was born into a show business family.

Her father, Lou Walters, who was Jewish, was born in London, England. After spending several years living in Belfast, Northern Ireland, Walters, along with his father and three brothers, immigrated to the United States and settled in New York City in 1909. Seven months later, Lou Walters's mother and his four sisters came to the United States as well.

Lou Walters was 15 years old when he arrived in New York City. As the oldest son, it fell to him to find a job to help support his family. Eager and ambitious, Lou would walk 3 miles (4.8 kilometers) every morning from the Lower East

Side of Manhattan to Times Square, where the day's want ads were posted in office windows. Competition for jobs was intense. For seven long months, Walters showed up for job interviews to find dozens of other boys there before him. He knew he would have to change his strategy.

On April 5, 1910, he saw an ad stating that Independent Booking Offices wanted an office boy. The ad said that applications would be accepted only after two o'clock that afternoon, but Lou was determined to get the job. He showed up at noon and convinced the desk clerk to get him in to see the boss, Mr. Stermdorf. Walters was forced to confess that he had no experience, he did not know how to type, and yes, he had read that applications were only accepted after two o'clock. Stermdorf sent him away, telling him to come back at two o'clock with everybody else.

Walters did return, convinced that he had blown his opportunity. Much to his surprise, though, the desk clerk and Stermdorf were waiting for him. Impressed by Walters's ambition, Stermdorf told him the job was his. It paid only six dollars a week, but that was six dollars more than Walters had ever earned before, and he jumped at the opportunity. Little did he know that it was the start of a career in show business that would last almost 60 years.

His job was to present the daily lists of his agency's clients to the people who booked entertainers for theatres and vaudeville halls, which allowed him to get a hands-on education in show business. He quickly proved his worth to his employer and did so well that when one of the owners of the agency moved to Boston to open a second office, he took Lou Walters with him.

Walters loved Boston and loved his job. Within a relatively short period of time, Walters left Independent Booking Offices and opened his own booking agency, the Lou Walters Booking Agency. He was on the road constantly, visiting vaudeville halls in small towns and large, searching for new and undiscovered talent.

He often found it. He discovered a young juggler named Fred Allen, who went on to become one of America's favorite comics, starring in theater, radio, and later television. He also discovered Jack Haley, another comedian who is best remembered today for his performance as the Tin Man in the classic 1939 film *The Wizard of Oz*. As a one-time penniless immigrant, Walters had come a long way and his booking agency was becoming one of the most powerful in the country. The money, as Barbara Walters described it in her memoir, was pouring in.

It was time for Lou Walters to find a wife. At a charity dance in Boston in 1919, he met Dena Seletsky, the granddaughter of Russian Jewish immigrants. With a father in poor health and six younger siblings to help support, Dena was working in a men's neckwear shop wrapping packages when she met Lou Walters. Just one year later, on May 30, 1920, they were married.

Walters bought his new bride a mink stole, and the newlyweds settled into married life in a 14-room mansion located in Newton, a suburb of Boston. Two years after the couple was married, Dena's father died of heart failure. Lou, always generous, invited the entire family, including Dena's sister, Lena, to live with them. When Lena married, her husband moved into the house as well. Soon, not only was the house filled with Dena's immediate family, but Dena and Lou began having a family of their own. Their firstborn child, a son named Burton, died of pneumonia in late 1922 at the age of one. A daughter, Jacqueline, was born in 1926.

By this time, the Walters family seemed to be sitting on top of the world. Lou Walters's booking agency was doing extraordinarily well—so well, in fact, that he could boast of owning two Cadillacs, a Pierce-Arrow, and

In this January 15, 1952, photo, Barbara Walters's father, Lou Walters (*right*), owner of the Latin Quarter, is shown with the Egyptian belly dancer and film actress Samia Gamal at the Latin Quarter in Miami Beach, Florida. At left is Gamal's husband, Sheppard King, a Texas oilman.

a Packard. Yet, by the time the family's second daughter, Barbara Jill Walters, was born on September 25, 1929, the mink stole had been sold, the four cars were gone, as was the 14-room mansion, and the family was learning to cope with a personal family misfortune for which there was no easy solution.

A ROLLER-COASTER CHILDHOOD

As Barbara Walters recalled in her memoir, *Audition*, her father had lost his fortune around the time she was born. At that time, no one in the Walters family could have predicted or prevented their financial difficulties.

There were several factors. The Great Depression, prompted by the stock market collapse of October 1929, was a worldwide economic downturn that affected individuals and businesses alike, including Walters's booking agency. But there was another event, one that happened on October 26, 1927, that shook the foundation of show business and changed the game forever. It was on that date that *The Jazz Singer*, the first feature-length motion picture with sound, premiered in New York City. Silent movies, which had been the norm since films had been invented, were out; "talkies" were in. And as more and more vaudeville halls were transformed into movie theaters, the age of live shows and vaudeville—the world Lou Walters had known so well—came to a screeching halt.

Lou Walters was forced to close his agency and had to resort to booking second- and even third-rate acts in tiny theaters that had not yet made the conversion to movies. It was a difficult time for the Walters family, made even more difficult as the Great Depression deepened through the 1930s. Lou was forced to travel up and down the East Coast of the United States with a company of performers and musicians, hoping to find a paying audience. Because he was so often away from home, young Barbara grew close to her mother and especially close to her older sister, Jacqueline.

There was something about Jacqueline that complicated their relationship, something that had an effect on the entire Walters family. Barbara delved into it in the introduction to her memoir:

> Jackie was three years older than I, but all our lives she appeared younger. My sister was mentally retarded, as the condition was called then, though only mildly so. Just enough to prevent her from attending regular school, from having friends, from getting a job, from marrying. Just enough to stop her from having a real life.
>
> Her condition also altered my life. I think I knew from a very early age that at some point Jackie would become my responsibility. That awareness was one of the main reasons I was driven to work so hard. But my feelings went beyond financial responsibility. For so many years I was embarrassed by her, ashamed of her, guilty that I had so much and she had so little. Very little was understood about retardation almost eighty years ago when Jackie was born.
>
> My parents protected her. They never discussed her outside the family or explained her condition to anyone. . . .
>
> Jackie's isolation also contributed to my own sense of isolation. . . . I rarely had friends over to the house because they didn't know what to make of my sister and I would hear the whispers—real or imagined.[1]

In that era, people with developmental disabilities were often not understood and did not have the opportunities that they do today to live as normal a life as possible. As Walters points out, there were very few schools then for the intellectually challenged and fewer places where they could learn a trade or work. While today it is likely that Jacqueline Walters could get a job, make friends outside the family, and perhaps even get married, she instead grew up isolated, protected from the outside world by her family members, who were doing what they felt at the time was the best thing for her.

But Jacqueline was not the only one being hurt by her family's protective attitude. Indeed, even at this early time in Barbara's life, one can see the two major influences that went into shaping her personality: her father's frequent absence due to the family's financial situation, and her sister's needs. (Her mother, naturally, needed to give more of her attention to Jacqueline, who could not always control her temper and needed help getting dressed and brushing her hair. Barbara, the "good" girl, did not need the attention, but she craved it nonetheless.) Combined, these two factors made Barbara feel she needed to prove herself and to provide for and to protect her sister and family.

A FINANCIAL UPSWING

In 1937, with just 63 cents to his name, Lou Walters took over the lease on a former Greek Orthodox Church in Boston. His dream was to build a nightclub that would rival the glamorous nightclubs of Paris, France, with their beautiful showgirls and top-notch entertainment. On October 1, 1937, Lou Walters opened his first in a series of nightclubs, the Latin Quarter.

There were two shows a night, with singers, acrobats, and comedians all performing their acts. The main attraction, however, was the line of chorus girls, who danced onstage in what were then considered skimpy costumes. Each show began with a theme song:

> So this is gay Pa-ree! Come on along with me.
> We're stepping out to see—the Latin Quarter.
> Put on your old beret. Let's sing the Marseillaise
> And put our wine away like water.[2]

With the Latin Quarter an immediate smash, financial success was once again Lou Walters's. The family soon moved to the middle-class Jewish neighborhood of Brookline, a suburb of Boston. Barbara attended the Lawrence Elementary School, where her fifth-grade teacher, Miss Gillis, described her as "a very serious pupil. . . . School was a place of business for her."[3]

Even though her father was successful, Walters was embarrassed both by her father's occupation as well as her parents' friends, who were largely people in the entertainment industry. Most of the other students at Lawrence were the children of professionals, and Barbara, not wanting to stand out in any way, wished that her father was something "respectable" like a doctor or a lawyer. (It was not until she was working as a young reporter that Barbara realized the benefit she had gained by growing up among show business celebrities. Having spent most of her life around them, she has never been starstruck or nervous while interviewing them.)

Evenings were often spent backstage at the Latin Quarter, doing her homework and watching over Jacqueline. Life was settling into a comfortable pattern for Barbara and her family, but Lou Walters was an ambitious man who was not content with running just one nightclub. He envisioned a chain of Latin Quarter nightclubs all across the country. So, at the age of 11, skinny and awkward (her relatives called her "Skinnymalinkydink"[4]), Barbara and her family left Massachusetts and their comfortable routine to set up shop in a new city.

ON THE MOVE

The family moved to Palm Island, Florida. A sparsely populated artificial strip of land connected only by a causeway to the cities of Miami and Miami Beach, it was where Lou Walters took a 10-year lease on a former nightclub and casino called the Palm Island Club. On December 13, 1940, the Lou Walters Miami Beach Latin Quarter opened and was a huge success, attracting both star performers and celebrity audience members.

Back on top of the show business heap once again, the Walters family moved into an enormous 15-room pistachio-green house on five acres (two hectares) of land sitting right on the water. Barbara not only had her own bedroom, she had her own playroom as well. It was, for the most part, a happy time for the entire family.

There were, of course, occasional problems. Because Barbara and Jacqueline were the only children living on Palm Island, Barbara had to be driven every day to elementary school across the causeway in Miami Beach. As a newcomer entering into school in the middle of the year, she found it difficult at first to fit in and make friends.

She did make one friend, though: Phyllis Fine, whose father was Larry Fine, of the famous comedy team the Three Stooges. Phyllis lived in a hotel in Miami, and on occasion, Barbara would spend the night there or Phyllis would spend the night in the pistachio-green house on Palm Island. But for the most part, because Palm Island was so isolated, Barbara spent much of her time alone, doing homework, reading, looking after Jacqueline, and spending her evenings backstage at the Latin Quarter.

But just when Barbara was getting adjusted to her new life, it was once again time to move. Lou Walters had picked the site for his next edition of the Latin Quarter. A great location had opened up on Broadway right on Times Square. But although Dena Walters was worried about the risk, there was never any doubt what Lou Walters's decision would be. In 1942, the Walters family moved to New York City.

Growing Up

Not surprisingly, the New York City version of the Latin Quarter was just as successful as those in Boston and Miami. It quickly became *the* club in New York, the place where the hottest celebrities went to watch Lou's celebrated chorus girls and some of America's most popular entertainers. A writer for the *Saturday Evening Post* wrote after the club's opening, "It became one of the most amazing operations in Broadway history."[1]

Although happy for her father's success, Barbara once again had to adjust to a new city, a new school, and new friends. She was enrolled in the exclusive Fieldston School in the Bronx, which was a magnet for the children of New York City's sophisticated and well-to-do Jewish families. Barbara, although a newcomer, soon became part of a close-knit circle of friends.

When not in school, the girls explored the city on their own, shopping in the best stores, going to movies and museums, riding their bicycles through Central Park. Barbara began, like other girls her age, to become interested in makeup, clothes, and dating. She felt, for perhaps the first time in her life, that she was part of a group, that she had real friends, and that she finally belonged.

There was, however, one difficulty: Jacqueline. Now a teenager, yet unable to attend school, Jacqueline spent her days with nothing to do. So, on those occasions when Barbara had plans to go out with friends, or even out on a date, her mother would beg her to take Jacqueline along. But Barbara—who truly loved her sister and felt guilty when Jacqueline stayed home alone, yet was embarrassed about Jacqueline's condition—gave in to her mother's requests as rarely as possible.

Walters described her conflicting feelings in her autobiography: "I loved my sister. She was sweet and affectionate and she was, after all, my sister. But there were times I hated her, too. For being different. For making *me* feel different. For the restraints she put on my life. I didn't like that hatred, but there's no denying that I felt it."[2] Decades later, Walters still feels guilt over this:

> I could be short or angry with her, and to this day I regret every harsh word I said to her. Why *didn't* I take my sister to the movies on a Saturday afternoon? There I was, her younger sister, with everything. And there was Jackie—with so little. The phone rang for me, but never for her. Friends came to see me, but not her.[3]

Barbara, always sensitive to being "different" and to "standing out," was also aware of the ways in which her family was different from others. Her father, always busy

A floorshow at Lou Walters's Latin Quarter nightclub in New York City on September 2, 1958. The move to New York, while successful for Lou Walters, proved to be an adjustment for a young Barbara Walters.

with the Latin Quarter, was on a different schedule from her friends' fathers. He worked nights, coming home after everyone else was asleep and waking up long after Barbara had gone to school. He was home for dinner only once a week, on Friday nights. Holidays and family birthdays were spent not at home, but down at the Latin Quarter.

After the family's first year in New York City, he was home less and less. Always ambitious, always willing to take risks, he tried to achieve the same success in Broadway theaters as he had in his nightclubs, opening up a series of expensive musical revues. But with the exception of his first attempt, the shows were not successful, and Walters lost a great deal of money.

Because of his financial losses, tension grew between Lou and Dena Walters, arguments of which Barbara was well aware. Then, for reasons that Walters is uncertain of to this day, her father made an announcement—they were moving back to Miami, much to her dismay.

The 15-room pistachio-green house was no longer available. The year was 1944, World War II was in full swing, and the U.S. Army was then using the house. The Latin Quarter was not the Latin Quarter anymore, either. It had been requisitioned by the army to feed new trainees. In its place, Lou Walters rented another club, the Colonial Inn, and the family settled into life on Hibiscus Island.

Barbara entered into high school sorority life, pledging at Lambda Pi. She started dating, threw parties by the pool, and was even chosen "Miss French Club." It was a good year, but with the end of the war in 1945, Lou Walters announced that, once again, it was time for the family to move. They were going back to New York City.

Once again, Walters's financial situation was on shaky ground. The Boston Latin Quarter had closed for good, and the New York City location had suffered financial losses during the war. But with the end of the war, the New York City Latin Quarter quickly became the undisputed king of nightclubs once again. The Palm Island Latin Quarter also reopened after the war's end and was soon filled with standing-room-only crowds.

The financial crisis averted, at least for the time being, the Walters family moved into a penthouse apartment looking over New York's Central Park. Barbara was accepted into a prestigious private school, Birch Wathen. Her life in New York was hardly that of a typical teenage girl—going to a private school, attending opening nights on Broadway with her famous father, summering at expensive resorts.

But, due to her father's latest ride on the financial roller coaster, she had come to a difficult realization for someone still so young. She became certain that her father could not be counted on to provide for her mother and sister, and that it would fall to her to provide her family with stability and financial security. A friend recalled Barbara telling her:

> "You can afford to be idealistic, but I have to do something in the real world." I remember very clearly her saying she had to have a career, that she really felt burdened by her retarded sister and her mother and father. She felt strongly she'd have to support them.
>
> Her attitude was tough, disciplined. . . . Barbara's family went from rags to riches a number of times. She knew she couldn't depend on her father, and that her mother and retarded sister couldn't depend on him for their old age. Barbara was a very intelligent girl, always. She was serious about responsibility.[4]

It was this sense of responsibility, this need to provide security for herself and her family, that would be the driving force throughout Barbara's life and career. At the same, though, just like any other high school girl, she desperately wanted to fit in with the rest of her class. She participated in after-school activities, such as exploring her talent for writing by working on the school's literary magazine, *Birch Leaves*. Her classmates remember her as being intelligent but introverted. Indeed, most of her socializing at the time was with old friends that she had made at the Fieldston School during her last stay in New York.

Upon high school graduation, Barbara applied to three colleges: Wellesley, one of the nation's finest all-women colleges; Pembroke College as her "safe" choice; and, finally, Sarah Lawrence, a fairly new all-women's college known for its progressive approach to education. At Sarah Lawrence, students created their own curriculum. There were no exams or grades; instead, students received written evaluations from their professors.

Of these, Barbara's first choice was Wellesley. But Wellesley put her on its waiting list, and Pembroke turned her down, so when Sarah Lawrence wrote to say that she was accepted, she was faced with a choice. Should she take a gamble and wait to see if Wellesley would ultimately have room for her? Or, should she go with Sarah Lawrence, the sure thing? Insecure and (unlike her father) unwilling to take any chances, she accepted the offer from Sarah Lawrence.

SARAH LAWRENCE

At 18 years old, Walters had no definite career goals in mind when she entered Sarah Lawrence. Perhaps because she had spent her life in a show business milieu, she took acting classes, even winning the lead role of Mary Boyle in the Sean O'Casey play *Juno and the Paycock*. She thrilled to the applause she received and for a time was certain that acting was in her future.

Indeed, she was so determined to be an actress that she considered dropping out of college to pursue her dreams. Her father went so far as to set up an audition for her, for an upcoming production of Tennessee Williams's *Summer and Smoke*. Two days before the audition, however, she reconsidered. As she said in her autobiography, "I knew, then, in my heart, that I didn't have the courage or the confidence to face being rejected, perhaps over and over. I was forced to face the fact that I wasn't going to be a great dramatic actress."[5]

Fortunately, she had taken other classes besides acting and had continued her writing career as the drama editor and movie critic for the college newspaper, the *Campus*. She had also easily settled into college social life, dating, making frequent trips into New York City with friends (the city is only half an hour away from Sarah Lawrence), getting elected president of her dormitory, and generally enjoying all that Sarah Lawrence had to offer.

Yet, for someone who would go on to become one of America's best-known journalists, she seemed, publicly at least, to be detached from the major issues of the day. Her college days were during the height of the Cold War, a time of continuous political conflict, military tension, and economic competition between the United States and the Communist government of the Soviet Union. Because of this ongoing tension, there was a nationwide fear of communism within the United States, today known as the "red scare." Many government hearings were held throughout the 1950s to weed out suspected Communists and those sympathetic to communism from all aspects of public life. Sarah Lawrence president Harold Taylor strongly objected to the requirement made by the House Committee on Un-American Activities (HUAC) and at the hearings held by Senator Joseph McCarthy of Wisconsin that those under

DID YOU KNOW?

While she was studying drama at Sarah Lawrence, one of Walters's favorite plays was Tennessee Williams's *The Glass Menagerie*. It tells the story of a Southern mother trying to find a suitable husband, a "gentleman caller," for her emotionally and physically frail daughter. But it is also the story of the son who is forced by his mother to help find those callers for his sister, and who eventually abandons his family and is overwhelmed with guilt over his decision. While not exactly like her situation, the emotional similarities were such that the play had (and still has) special meaning for Walters.

Senator Joseph McCarthy *(left)* covers the microphones to have a whispered discussion with his chief counsel, Roy Cohn, during a committee hearing in Washington, D.C., on April 26, 1954. Barbara Walters dated Cohn while she attended Sarah Lawrence College. Although many of her classmates disapproved of their relationship, she was grateful for Cohn's help in getting her father out of some legal difficulties.

investigation be forced to sign loyalty oaths to the American government.

Although many students and faculty at Sarah Lawrence and other colleges and universities nationwide rallied against the government's tactics, Walters remained apolitical. Indeed, it was at this time that she first began dating Assistant U.S. Attorney Roy Cohn, who was then chief counsel to Joseph McCarthy. Walters, though, seemed oblivious to the implications of dating a man whose political views were so far opposed to those of most of Sarah Lawrence's student body. In response, a cartoon in the school's yearbook portrayed her as an ostrich with her head in the sand, unwilling or unable to see what was going on around her.

On weekends, she would often go home to visit her family. Life there, though, was depressing for Walters. Her father was generally away, traveling back and forth between New York and Miami Beach. This left her mother and sister on their own most of the time. So, almost every night, Dena and Jacqueline would go to the movies—anything to pass the time.

But then came a miracle—television. Jacqueline loved having one of the new televisions in their house, particularly because many of the entertainers she saw on TV were those she knew from their performances at the Latin Quarter. Ironically, while TV proved to be a blessing for Jacqueline, it was the beginning of the end of Lou Walters's show-business career. As more and more people stayed home to watch television, fewer and fewer were willing to get dressed up to go out to watch scantily-clad showgirls perform live onstage.

In 1951, Barbara Walters graduated from Sarah Lawrence with a degree in English. Her friends all seemed to have their futures laid out. One was going to run an art gallery, another was going to be a social worker, and several were going to earn their advanced degrees. Walters, on the other hand, was still in the same place she had been when she entered college, with nothing that she really wanted to do and nothing in particular she thought she was any good at.

She returned home to plan her future. On a passing bus, she saw an ad that read, "If u cn red ths, u can ern mo pa."[6] So, despite having earned her degree from Sarah Lawrence, Barbara Walters decided to continue her education at a Speedwriting school on New York's Forty-second Street.

Finding Her Way

Walters aced her Speedwriting class, ranking at the top of 83 students. But despite this sterling accomplishment, for the next 10 years, her life was one of constant changes, both professional and personal, as she tried to find her own way into adult life.

Consider this: She was offered her first job not because of her degree from Sarah Lawrence or because of her skill at Speedwriting, but because the advertising man who was going behind her up the stairs to an employment agency liked her legs. As Walters points out in her autobiography, that kind of behavior is frowned upon today, but then it was often the norm. And since she had no other offers and did not want to go to graduate school, she took him up on his offer. Besides, as she says proudly, she *did* have great legs!

She had worked at the advertising agency for a year when a friend told her of an opening in the publicity department at WNBT, an affiliate station of NBC. There was one problem—she had never worked in publicity before in her life. (People in the publicity department of a company are responsible for sending out press releases regarding upcoming events to media outlets, hoping that the media outlets will then do stories on those events.)

Although Walters had never worked in publicity, she did have a father who had been in show business nearly all his life. So, besides listing her skills in Speedwriting and typing on her résumé, she mentioned the fact that she was the daughter of Lou Walters and had grown up knowing most of New York's most powerful Broadway columnists. Needless to say, she got the job.

It was an invaluable learning experience for her. In no time, she was writing up to six press releases a day. And when not writing releases, Walters would call the columnists personally. Owing to who she was, they not only took her calls, but she also got a large number of items about the station's shows written about in newspaper columns that appeared nationwide. Although it sometimes had its drawbacks, being the daughter of Lou Walters could have its advantages as well.

Additionally, through a training program run by the station, she got the chance to learn how to produce a television show as well as hone her writing skills. Walters worked on a 15-minute daily children's program called *Ask the Camera*. (The show's director was a young man named Roone Arledge, who years later would become the head of ABC News and Walters's boss.)

The show's format was simple. People would send in questions, which were answered on the air using clips from the station's film library. Not only did Walters produce the show, she also wrote the voice-over narration and learned to edit the film to fit into the allotted time. As she said in her autobiography, "I got so good at it that eventually I didn't need to use a stopwatch. I could both write copy and edit film almost to the second. I still can."[1]

By learning to write copy and edit film, she absorbed the basics that went into telling a good story on television—specifically, that if there is a strong beginning and an equally powerful ending, the middle section of the story does not have to be dramatic. It is a narrative formula that she still uses today.

While the show may seem rather basic and simple by today's standards, back then, the fact that a woman was producing the show was enough to get it noticed. The May 15, 1953, issue of *TV Guide* had an article about Walters titled "Young Producer," calling her one of "the bright young people in responsible jobs"[2] in television. It would be the first of many such stories in Walters's long career.

Although Walters was 24 years old and working full-time, she was still living in her parents' home, like most young, single women of the era. This is not to say, of course, that she was not dating. For nearly a year, she dated Ted Cott, her boss at WNBT, an older man with two children who was in the midst of getting a divorce. But after that relationship began to fade and she started dating other men while still working with Cott, Walters found herself forced to leave WNBT and go in search of another job.

She landed a job on *The Eloise McElhone Show*. Although her official title was executive producer, in reality she did it all: associate producer, writer, script girl, guest booker, and even coffee maker! In those early days of television, there was an atmosphere of experimentation, and with half an hour to fill daily, the show had a little bit of everything, ranging from interviews with guests to exercise and cooking demonstrations and even advice about pets and relationships. While the work was hard,

In this May 25, 1954, photo, Liberace plays a mini piano for the benefit of Ona Munson *(center)* and Eloise McElhone on *The Eloise McElhone Show*, one of the first television programs a young Barbara Walters worked on.

she learned the ins and outs of producing a television show from every angle.

It was because of this experience that today, when Walters is asked by young people how to break into television, she advises them to:

> [G]o to your local television stations, take any job that's offered, and work your fanny off. Volunteer for everything without looking at the time clock. Learn how it all works. Crises happen. Producers don't show up. Guests don't show up. Scripts are lost. Be in place.[3]

With *The Eloise McElhone Show* on summer hiatus, Walters went to Europe with a friend. While there, she learned that the show would not be returning in the fall. She was, once again, out of a job. After spending time traveling and even doing a bit of modeling in Paris, Walters, unemployed, returned home to Florida to visit her parents and sister. It was there that she met the man who would become her first husband.

NEWLYWED

His name was Bob Katz, a good-looking, athletic man whose father was then the country's largest manufacturer of children's hats. Her family liked him, and her friends liked him. Although Walters herself had doubts about their relationship, she married him after a short engagement in June 1955. After the honeymoon was over, the two returned to New York City to begin their life as newlyweds.

Walters quickly learned that being a stay-at-home wife was not for her. Bored and unhappy, she and Bob came to the conclusion that for the good of their marriage, Barbara would return to work. (At this time, it was extremely rare for the wife of a fairly successful man to work. By encouraging his wife to get a job, Bob proved to be a man ahead of his time.)

Walters quickly landed a job on CBS's *The Morning Show*. Hosted by the young newscaster Walter Cronkite and the still largely unknown comic actor Dick Van Dyke, it also featured a "weather girl," a sportscaster, and a pair of puppets that performed to popular songs. The program was the network's attempt to compete with NBC's ratings powerhouse, *The Today Show*. Barbara's job was to write and produce segments, largely regarding fashion, to help attract female viewers.

Up against *The Today Show*, the show tried everything it could to increase its ratings. For a period, the weather report was done by a young woman in a bathing suit in a glass tank who drew circles on a map to show the areas being forecast. Another time, an archery champion was brought in to shoot arrows into a large map of the United States while Dick Van Dyke read the weather report.

Nothing seemed to help the show's ratings, but Walters, now 26, was beginning to get noticed. *Morning Show* producer Charlie Andrew remembered her as "ambitious, determined. You could see it in her eyes."[4] And feature coordinator Madeline Amgott observed, "She always knew she wanted to be in front of the camera."[5]

In 1956, CBS changed *The Morning Show* into a new show called *Good Morning!*, with Will Rogers Jr. as host. Despite the change, ratings were still low. Walters gave it her all, getting up every morning at four o'clock to arrive at the studio in her role as talent booker and all-around behind the scenes go-to idea person. One morning, though, when a bathing suit model failed to show up, Walters was drafted to take her place. It was her network television debut!

A major step in her career development occurred on July 26, 1956. On that date, the Italian luxury liner *Andrea Doria* collided with the Swedish ship *Stockholm* in dense fog off the coast of Nantucket, Massachusettes. Forty-six people were killed, but many others were saved. The producer of *Good Morning!*, Av Westin, asked Walters to go to the pier that night to see if she could convince some of the survivors of the tragedy to appear on the show the next morning to be interviewed.

It was her first experience dealing with that kind of traumatic situation. Imagine what it must have been like, approaching people who had just been saved from a sinking ship, and saying to them, "What a horrible experience you've been through. You must be feeling terrible. But could you come into our studio tomorrow morning at 7:00

A.M. to tell us about it?"[6] Surprisingly, a good number of them agreed to be interviewed.

Such an approach raises an interesting question about reporting and ethics: Was Walters exploiting the suffering of others by requesting interviews with survivors? Or is it only through hearing their stories that the viewer can truly appreciate and understand the tragedy of what they went through? Most reporters must ask themselves such questions, and by and large, they conclude that the public has the right to know the truth of any news story, as seen by those who were part of it.

Walters's success in obtaining interviews proved to her bosses that she was an aggressive and determined reporter with a great future. That future, though, would not be with *Good Morning!* Soon after her *Andrea Doria* success, the show was canceled. She was assigned to another project, as a writer for a series titled *The Day That. . .* , which would explore in depth what happened on, for example, the day that President Franklin Roosevelt died. That show, too, was canceled, before a single show appeared on the air.

THINGS GET WORSE

For the first time in her adult life, Walters was forced to go on unemployment. She was also faced with a series of difficult personal events. Her marriage to Bob Katz came to a quiet end when, after three years of marriage, the couple decided to divorce. As if that were not enough, her father's finances were, once again, taking a terrifying plunge.

Lou Walters, who had been having difficulties with his business partner at the Latin Quarter for years, sold his shares and walked away from the club, determined to open a new club that would be even bigger and better. That club, Café de Paris, opened in May 1958. A month later, it was closed, and Lou Walters was bankrupt.

He was forced to sell everything: his Fifth Avenue apartment, his library, and his art collection. With his life crumbling around him, he attempted suicide in June 1958. After he recovered, he made plans to move down to the family's Florida home with his wife and daughter Jacqueline, but that house was soon seized for back taxes, and the three were forced to find a small apartment in Miami Beach. Suddenly, it seemed possible that Lou might end up in prison. But thanks to the help of Barbara's old beau Roy Cohn, the charges were dropped.

It was an extremely difficult period for Barbara. Her worst childhood fear had come true: She was now responsible not only for herself, but for her father, mother, and sister as well. "I knew I'd have to work all my life so I'd never feel financial pressure,"[7] she said years later in an interview.

Unable to find work in television, she got a $60-a-week job at a public relations firm called Tex McCrary. Her job was to write press releases to convince radio and television producers to use the company's clients as guests on their shows. Her boss there was William Safire, who later became a speechwriter for President Richard Nixon, a Pulitzer Prize–winning columnist for the *New York Times*, and a best-selling author.

Walters learned a lot writing press releases and client profiles for television and radio producers. It was excellent training for someone whose livelihood would soon depend on landing interviews from newsmakers and celebrities. But while her job may sound glamorous, at that time she lived in a small apartment, took the bus to the office, worked hard, and then came home to eat a bologna sandwich for dinner.

She worked at Tex McCrary for five years before deciding in 1961 that it was time for her to move on. She went

to an employment agency and soon got an offer to work at
Redbook. Not happy about the magazine job but ready for
a change, she took the offer. And it was there at *Redbook*,
bored and unhappy, that she got the call from her old boss
at *The Morning Show*, Fred Freed. Despite the fact that the
job offer was only temporary, she jumped at the chance to
return to television, even as a writer. In just three years, she
would be on the air full-time and on her way to becoming
one of the most famous television journalists in the world.

Making It in a
Man's World

As previously mentioned, Walters's career on *Today* began as a producer and writer for five-minute segments, aired five days a week, with Anita Colby for S&H Green Stamps. She was so good at what she was doing that when Colby's segment was renewed after the first three-month period, so was Walters's.

She was earning just a couple of hundred dollars a week, but she was back in the industry that she loved. But after the second three-month period, S&H Green Stamps decided not to continue its five-minute spots on *Today*. Once again, Walters was left wondering if she was still going to have a job. But this time, unlike at CBS, lady luck decided to smile on her.

Today kept a stable of eight writers, one of whom was female. Shortly after Colby's segments stopped, that female writer left the show to get married. Walters was willing, available, and there. Fred Freed hired her to work full-time as a writer, writing specifically for the *Today* Girl. But a chain of events was about to begin that would change both her role and responsibilities.

MOVING UP

When Dave Garroway, the show's host since its inception, left the show, he was replaced by NBC News correspondent John Chancellor, who brought with him Shad Northshield as the show's new producer. Chancellor, a well-respected journalist, did not quite fit in as a host of a morning show and lasted only 14 months. But the show's new producer, while lasting only as long as Chancellor, put changes into effect that considerably raised Walters's career profile.

"I don't see what Barbara is doing just writing women's features," he remarked at a meeting. "She's perfectly capable of writing any of the stories for the show."[1] And with that, for the first time in the history of *Today*, a female writer was given writing assignments that were not directly related to so-called women's stories. As Walters said in her autobiography, "Did the world stop? Did anyone realize what was happening?"[2] To this the answer, obviously, was, no.

Her workday was a long one. Up at four A.M. Meet with John Chancellor in the studio and go over the morning's interviews. Meet with the guests to go over the kinds of questions they would be asked. Attend the after-the-show meeting to go over what went right and what went wrong with that morning's show. Grab a sandwich. Go to her office to book guests for upcoming shows. Write features and questions for future interviews. At six P.M., take the bus home, grab a bologna sandwich from the deli across the street from her apartment, and be in bed by nine-thirty. Repeat five days a week.

Her hard work did not go unnoticed. In July 1961, she made her on-air debut, sitting on a bicycle to introduce a piece on bike riding in New York City's Central Park. Not the most glamorous of debuts, but good enough to earn her another assignment—a trip to Paris, France, to cover the new fall fashion collections.

Today, Walters proudly owns the black-and-white film of her August 29, 1961, assignment sitting at *The Today Show* desk. Getting to go to Paris to cover women's fashions and then come back to New York to introduce her reports live on the air was not the most demanding of assignments. And, although she loved doing the segment, she claims that she never dreamed that she would become a regular on-air personality herself. All she wanted to do was whatever it took for her to keep her job. As she explained in her auto-biography, job insecurity would be a driving force in her life for many years to come:

> For the next twenty years, thirty years, maybe even forty, I would feel the same way. No matter how high my profile became, how many awards I received, or how much money I made, my fear was that it all could be taken away from me. It doesn't take a rocket scientist to link that insecurity to my father's roller-coaster career or to my mother's constant anxiety about my sister's needs. I have, as I've said, always felt I was auditioning, either for a new job or to make sure that I could hold on to the one I had.[3]

Fortunately, it was a relatively stable time for her and her family. Her father, mother, and sister were living in Las Vegas, where Lou Walters was making a brief show-business comeback, producing lavish shows with the high production values and showgirls he loved so much. As for

In this early 1960s photo, television journalists *(left to right)* Jack Lescoulie, Hugh Downs, Barbara Walters, and Frank Blair conduct a discussion in the *Today* show studio in New York City. It was the start of her enormously successful broadcast journalism career.

Barbara, she was about to start out on the most high-profile assignment of her career thus far.

In March 1962, Jacqueline Kennedy, the wife of President John F. Kennedy, departed on a goodwill trip to India and Pakistan. Forty-five reporters from around the country were selected to cover the first lady's trip. Of these, seven were women: six from newspapers and magazines, and one from television, the largely inexperienced Barbara Walters. How was she selected? *The Today Show* saw the trip as largely a woman's story, and since Walters could both write and report, they felt she was the perfect (and most cost-effective) reporter for the job.

She covered every aspect of Mrs. Kennedy's appearances, from her visit to a hospital for the poor in New Delhi, to a visit to the Taj Mahal, to elephant rides accompanied by the first lady's sister, Lee Radziwill. Not only that, but Walters also got the opportunity to obtain interviews with the area's leaders, including ones with President Ayub Khan of Pakistan and Indira Gandhi, the daughter of Prime Minister Jawaharlal Nehru of India, who would later become her nation's prime minister.

Even at this early stage in her career, Walters was bridging the gap between "entertainment" reporting and "hard-news" reporting—covering everything from the size of Jacqueline Kennedy's shoes (size 10) to politics in Pakistan. It is this ability and willingness to do both that has earned her both praise and criticism throughout her career.

Despite her best efforts, her hard work was going largely unnoticed back in the United States. To get the network's attention, she would have to do something special. So she set out to win a private interview with Jacqueline Kennedy herself, becoming the only reporter on the tour to do so.

How did she do it? Aware that her reports were not getting enough air time, and worried about her career, she went to Letitia Baldridge, Kennedy's social secretary, for help and told her, "I'm going to be fired, I'm going to be ruined,"[4] and that she needed the interview in order to save her job. It worked. Baldridge approached the first lady, telling her: "You've got to give this girl a chance, otherwise she's going to go home in disgrace. She's going to be fired. She's going to go home with nothing—no special footage of you."[5] Kennedy agreed, and Walters got an exclusive interview. Baldridge added: "It was such a victory for Barbara. She really came home a success."[6]

Her hard work had finally been noticed, in particular by *Today*'s producer, Al Morgan, who recalled:

Barbara Walters was a fine writer. We let her do the fashion pieces and occasional women's pieces. One of the first high points of her career was when she went to India with Jacqueline Kennedy. After that I began to use her on other assignments. I really respected her. She learned how to edit film, score a story, get the story on the air. I feel I raised Barbara from a cub.[7]

Careers, however, are a funny thing. Despite the success of her trip, it is possible her career would not have gone to the next level if there had not been another shake-up on *Today*. Faced with slumping ratings, NBC dropped John Chancellor, replacing him with Hugh Downs. Downs, a popular game-show host and former sidekick to *The Tonight Show*'s host Jack Paar, was one of NBC's most popular talents. Downs, in turn, became one of Walters's biggest allies and supporters.

He urged the show's producer to use her more often, substituting Walters for *Today* Girl actress Pat Fontaine. As she got more airtime, she became more confident in her abilities. She learned to speak more slowly, to smile more, to become more relaxed and less intense during interviews. She learned, as she has said, to "lighten up" on camera. All she needed now was her big break. She got it on one of the most tragic days in America's history.

THE KENNEDY ASSASSINATION

When President John F. Kennedy was assassinated while riding in a motorcade in Dallas, Texas, on Friday, November 22, 1963, the United States and the entire world were stunned. For the next four days, all eyes were glued to television sets as the networks, for the first time in history, began around-the-clock coverage of a news event.

Because all reporters were needed for around-the-clock coverage, Walters was sent to Washington, D.C., to cover the arrival of the president's coffin at the Capitol building. At one point, she was on the air for five straight hours, reporting on the lines of people, both known and unknown, who were waiting to pay their respects. It was the first time she had reported on a national news event, and she passed the test with flying colors. *Today* show producer Al Morgan called it her coming-of-age as a reporter.

At the same time that her career was really beginning to take off, her personal life took an unexpected turn. For two years, she had been dating Lee Guber, a producer and theatre owner, nine years her senior. In the summer of 1963, the couple had announced their engagement. But Walters had strong reservations about marrying a man who, like her father, was willing to gamble everything that his next show was going to be a hit. Three months into the engagement, she broke it off.

But a few days after she returned home from covering Kennedy's funeral, Guber came to her door and announced that life was too short and that they should get married immediately. Walters, for whom Kennedy's assassination had also stirred thoughts on how one's life can change in a second, agreed. On December 8, 1963, just two weeks after the assassination, Barbara Walters and Lee Guber were married.

The new Mrs. Guber was not, as she had attempted to be during her first marriage, going to settle for being "just" a housewife. When she learned that Pat Fontaine was going to be let go from her role as the *Today* Girl, Walters lobbied furiously for the job. Instead, to her great disappointment, the job was given to film and Broadway actress Maureen O'Sullivan, today best remembered for her role as Jane in the early Tarzan movies and as mother of actress Mia Farrow.

It turned out, however, that the skills needed to be an actress are often very different than the ones required on a morning television show. In film or onstage, O'Sullivan had a script to read and a role to play. On television, she had to be able to be herself for two hours of live television, in addition to being able to interview people from all walks of life. In the end, the role of *Today* Girl was not a good match for O'Sullivan. Within months, she was gone, and the position of *Today* Girl was once again up for grabs. Hugh Downs, always Walters's biggest supporter, urged that she be given the job. NBC executives, though, had their doubts.

Walters, while a very attractive woman, did not fit the usual mold of the *Today* Girl beauty. Despite her many appearances on the show, she was still not widely known. There was also the problem of her voice. Walters not only had a noticeable Boston accent, she had an even more noticeable problem pronouncing the letter *r*. Why, executives asked, should they take a chance?

Yet there were factors in her favor. NBC knew Walters and knew the quality of her work. There was also an additional consideration: As opposed to hiring a known celebrity, they could hire her for cheap. With Downs's backing, Walters assumed a new role as the *Today* Girl in October 1964. She would not, however, hold the job alone: Walters would appear on the air three days a week, alternating with Judith Crist, a well-known movie critic, and Aline Saarinen, an art critic and widow of the famous Finnish-born architect Eero Saarinen.

Within months though, it became obvious that viewers liked her, the show's sponsors liked her, and Downs and the rest of the *Today* team liked her as well. The job was hers alone. And as a bonus (and as a nod to the growing women's rights movement), Walters would no longer be called the *Today* Girl. Instead, she would be called the new *Today* reporter. Her career was about to jump into overdrive.

TODAY

No longer just a writer, Walters received a new contract that would earn her $700 a week (a sizable income for the time) along with a slew of benefits, including chauffeured cars to and from the studio (no more buses for her!), her own office and secretary, and a personal budget that required her to hire a business team to handle her finances. And, knowing from her years working in public relations the value of staying in the public eye, she hired a public relations firm to help promote her name and generate additional media coverage.

It worked. During her first year in her new role, article after laudatory article appeared celebrating NBC's "new" news reporter. In *Life*, she was praised as the rising star of NBC in an article with a headline that read "Barbara Walters of '*Today*' Show Looks Sharp—and Is Early to Rise, Wealthy and Wise." She was even invited by Johnny Carson to appear on NBC's popular late-night program, *The Tonight Show*.

As a woman in television news, she was a novelty. So, while the headline of a profile of her in the *New York Herald Tribune* read "They Love Her in the Morning," in the story, the author was happy to point out that, although she was doing traditionally a "man's" role, "That Barbara Walters is a girl no one can deny."[8] Noted feminist Gloria Steinem wrote about her in an article for the *New York Times*, "Nylons in the Newsroom." In the piece, Steinem praised Walters for being a "new" kind of woman on television, one not hired for her beauty and glamour, but for her talent. Walters herself is quoted in the article as saying, "I'm a kind of well-informed friend. They don't want me to be a glamour puss and that's fine. It means I won't have to quit or have face lifts after 40. I'm in a different category."[9]

Her newfound fame, along with her father's name and connections, made it easier for her to book interviews with other famous people. She became known as the show's unofficial celebrity interviewer, landing interviews with such notables as legendary dancer Fred Astaire, singer and film star Judy Garland, author Truman Capote, and actor Warren Beatty. Beatty proved to be so difficult a subject that after trying to get him to answer the simple question, "Mr. Beatty, what is your new movie about?" and failing to get an answer, Walters declared on live television, "Mr. Beatty, you are the most difficult interview I've ever had. We'll go to a commercial."[10]

She interviewed other kinds of celebrities—Golda Meir, the Israeli prime minister, and Kathleen Cleaver, the wife of Black Panther leader Eldridge Cleaver—as well, and got many of them to reveal many surprising things on the air. Mamie Eisenhower, for example, told Walters that the secret of her 50-year marriage to the former president, Dwight D. Eisenhower, was that "We have absolutely nothing in common."[11] When Walters asked Rose Kennedy, the matriarch of the Kennedy political clan and mother of two murdered sons, President John F. Kennedy and Senator Robert F. Kennedy, what gave her the strength to cope with the loss of her children, she answered, "I just made up my mind that I was not going to be vanquished."[12]

One interview often turned into another. While interviewing Tricia Nixon in the Rose Garden of the White House, Tricia's father, President Richard Nixon, approached Walters and introduced himself. The two briefly discussed an upcoming dinner that Nixon was hosting for Great Britain's Prince Philip, and Nixon asked Walters if she was going to interview him. Walters replied that she had tried to get an interview with the prince, but with no luck. Nixon promised to speak to Prince Philip, and later that night, the interview was hers.

Richard Nixon was not her only fan in high places. Dean Rusk, secretary of state in the Kennedy and Johnson administrations, took it upon himself to write her a fan letter in August 1967. In it, he told her how much he admired her work and added, "If NBC Vice Presidents ever begin to bother you, show them this letter and others like it and tell them to leave you alone."[13] When Rusk resigned his office at the end of Lyndon Johnson's presidency in January 1969, Walters was granted an exclusive three-part interview that won her both critical acclaim and the envy of her colleagues.

Although she was becoming known for her celebrity interviews, she worked and reported on other kinds of stories as well. Her stories were as varied as her interests: For example, she attended *Playboy* magazine president Hugh Hefner's "bunny school," where aspiring young women went to learn the skills needed to work in his clubs. (Walters even worked tables in the full bunny costume at one of the clubs, all to get the firsthand experience necessary for her to effectively tell the story of the other women who worked there.) She reported from the 1968 Democratic Convention in Chicago, where she could smell the tear gas used by Mayor Richard Daley's police force to break up antiwar demonstrations. She reported about the life of a Marymount nun. Wherever there was a news story waiting to be told, Barbara Walters was there.

In addition to her work on *Today*, Walters contributed to two NBC radio programs, *Monitor* and *Emphasis*. Based on her skills as an interviewer, she wrote a bestselling book, *How to Talk with Practically Anybody About Practically Anything*. (Although, according to some reports, Canadian journalist June Callwood actually wrote it, based on Walters's ideas and her original outline.) Walters also contributed regularly to such popular magazines as *Ladies' Home Journal*, *Good Housekeeping*, and *Reader's Digest*. And to top it off, in 1971, she began hosting a five-day-a-week half-hour interview program.

Barbara Walters carries her daughter, Jacqueline, near Central Park in New York City in the early 1970s. Although she loved being a mother, managing her career and raising a child at the same time often proved difficult for Walters.

The television show began its life with the name *For Women Only*. Hosted by Aline Saarinen (one of the three rotating *Today* Girls before Walters took over the position full-time), it was an intellectually challenging panel show that immediately followed *Today* in many cities. But while the show was critically acclaimed, not many women wanted to watch intellectuals and academics discuss various high-brow topics at nine o'clock in the morning. So, when Saarinen decided to leave the program to go to Paris to become NBC's first female bureau chief, the network asked Walters to take over.

The newly revamped show, *Not for Women Only*, pre-miered in September 1971. Instead of discussing cultural trends, the emphasis was broadened to include topics such as "Is the Family Dying?" and "TV and Children." Within six months, not only had the program's ratings tripled, but the *New York Times* called *Not for Women Only* "one of the most improved and provocative shows in the entire early morning schedule."[14] With another hit on her hands, Walters found herself with an even higher public profile.

To accommodate Walters's already frantic working schedule, it was arranged that an entire week's worth of *Not for Women Only* programs would be taped in one evening, one right after the other. This was essential to Walters, because by this point in her life, she was not only a woman at the top of her career, but also a wife and mother.

DID YOU KNOW?

As is the case with many mother-daughter relationships, Jacqueline and Barbara Walters went through a very difficult period during Jacqueline's teenage years. Jacqueline struggled with the problems of growing up as the child of a famous and often absent mother. Often wondering whether her friends liked her for herself or because of her mother, Jacqueline had considerable self-esteem issues and ended up experimenting with drugs and even running away from school to hitchhike across the country. Barbara tried to help her daughter, despite being racked with guilt about how her fame and absences may have contributed to her daughter's problems.

Today, their relationship is strong, and Jacqueline opened a residential therapy program for girls with problems similar to hers, New Horizons for Young Women, which closed in 2008 due to economic difficulties.

NOT JUST A CAREER WOMAN

In 1968, Walters, at age 39, and her husband decided to adopt a child. The couple had tried for years to have a child of their own, but after suffering through three miscarriages, they adopted a girl named Jacqueline. Walters hoped that by naming her "Jacqueline" after her sister, it would ease her sister's unhappiness at not having any children of her own.

Walters loved being a mother. Thirty years after adopting Jacqueline, she spoke to *McCall's* about what it meant to her: "She is what makes it a home. I wanted a child *very very* badly. You have to want a child very badly if you're in this business. I made the choice. I was not young; I had a career."[15] Of course, unlike most other working mothers, Walters was able to afford live-in staff to be with Jacqueline when she could not be there herself.

Like many other working mothers, Walters also felt a great deal of guilt when she was not able to be there. Still, she spent as much time with her daughter as she could. And, when it came time to explain to her that she had been adopted, she knew just how to tell her while reassuring her just how much she loved her. "Some babies come from their mommies' tummies," she told her. "But you, my darling, you were born in my heart."[16]

In the fall of 1971, America's best-known female journalist was making $2,500 a week on *The Today Show*, was hosting *Not for Women Only*, and had recently won an exclusive interview with President Richard Nixon. She was happy in her role as wife and mother and was relieved to be able to support her father, mother, and sister, now back living in Miami. She seemed to have it all. But a decision was being made that would not only change her role at *The Today Show* but force her to again fight battles she thought had long been resolved.

Difficulties

For several years, Barbara Walters had been working alongside Hugh Downs and former baseball star Joe Garagiola (who had joined the show in 1967) on *Today* in a working relationship that was warm, friendly, and supportive. In her autobiography, Walters recalled that "those four years with Hugh and Joe were among the happiest years of my forty-years-and-counting tenure on television. The three of us appreciated one another's respective talents, and rather than compete, we made one another look good. This would not always be the case for me with other partners in the future, which is why I remember those years with such fondness."[1]

And indeed, those years came to a crashing halt in the fall of 1971, when Downs, one of Barbara Walters's biggest fans and supporters, decided to leave *The Today Show* after nine years as host. While today it may seem surprising that Walters was never considered as a possible replacement, network executives then thought that she was still "just" a reporter and that hosting a program such as *Today* was for men only.

The show's new host would be Frank McGee, a well-respected television reporter and news anchor. McGee, however, did not particularly like working on *Today*, which he considered a step down from his previous job as one of the anchors for NBC's evening news. He also felt that women had no place reporting anything that could be considered "serious" news.

Troubles erupted on the set early in McGee's tenure. He had instituted a daily series of interviews with news-makers and politicians in New York City and Washington, D.C., during which he and Walters sat side by side and took turns asking questions. But McGee had a problem with that. He felt that his questions were more important than hers and that her questions were simply unneeded interruptions. The show's producer, however, liked the format and ignored McGee's complaints. So McGee went straight to the top, complaining to NBC president Julian Goodman.

A meeting was called between Goodman, McGee, and Walters. McGee told Goodman in no uncertain terms that Walters's participation in the interviews diminished their importance. He argued, again, with Walters sitting in the room and listening to every word, that her role should be restricted to what he called "girlie" interviews. It would be fine with him, he told Goodman, if she remained sitting at the desk, but not if she actually joined in the conversation. Much to Walters's shock and dismay, Goodman did not dismiss McGee's argument. Instead, he agreed with McGee that her role on the show would have to be diminished.

In this January 12, 1972, photo, *(from left to right)* Gene Shalit, Joe Garagiola, Barbara Walters, and Frank McGee appear on *Today*, on the day of Garagiola's final appearance on the program. Walters loved working with Garagiola but had difficulties with McGee.

Despite her ongoing insecurities and her gratitude that she had a job of any kind, Walters stood up for herself. She told the NBC president that she had not worked on the show for as long as she had, and contributed all the news-making, ground-breaking interviews she had done, to be pushed back into the role of the *Today* Girl. In her autobiography, *Audition*, Walters wrote: "I consider that day to be one of the milestones of my career. I cannot imagine what my future would have been had I just swallowed my feelings and restricted my work to the 'girlie' assignments."[2]

Instead, a compromise was reached: Walters could still take part in the daily interviews with the powerful and famous, but McGee would have the right to ask the first three questions. Only when he had finished, and only if there was enough time remaining, would she have the right to ask a fourth question. More significantly, McGee reserved the right to interview anybody he wanted to—without Walters. If a guest came to the studio for an interview, and McGee wanted to do it, it was his. Her fate, her role on the show, was entirely in his hands. Walters, naturally, was furious, her anger only heightened by the fact that McGee was earning twice her salary.

In public, she smiled and played nice, telling reporters, "I'm there to be there if Frank wants someone to turn to for help in an interview."[3] In private though, she was looking for an opening, a way to work *around* Frank McGee's demands and still do the job she wanted to do. Finally, she figured it out.

The agreement had been that McGee had first rights to interview anyone who came into the studio. But no one had said that Walters could not get interviews on her own and conduct them *outside* the studio. She went to work, adding additional newspapers and magazines to her already crowded reading lists, searching for interesting people who were in the news who might make for a good interview.

Then it would be up to her to go out and get the interview. Walters hated making phone calls, so she instead wrote prospective interviewees personal letters. In them, she would not discuss why she wanted to do the interview. Instead, she would tell them why they should want to do the interview. By sitting down with her, she would patiently explain, they would have the opportunity to let the public know their side of the story.

A good early example of this strategy was her interview with Henry Ford II, who at the time was the president of the Ford Motor Company. An intensely private man, he had never given a television interview. But he and his company had recently been in the news after noted consumer advocate Ralph Nader attacked Ford's company for unsafe practices in building its cars. Walters wrote one letter to Ford suggesting that an interview would allow him to tell his side of the story, then wrote a second letter strongly suggesting one.

Needless to say, she got the interview. Her persistence and hard work paid off, and the stream of headline-making interviews continued. Everybody from 94-year-old conductor Leopold Stokowski, First Lady Patricia Nixon, National Security Advisor Henry Kissinger, and presidential aide H.R. Haldeman sat down with Walters to tell their stories directly to the viewing audience.

Of course, it was Walters's job not only to let the interviewee talk, but to ask the tough questions that needed to be answered. In her interview with Haldeman, for example, she asked him what kind of criticisms upset the president. At the time, the Nixon administration was in negotiations with the leadership in North Vietnam to end the Vietnam War. Haldeman took the opportunity to insist that those who opposed what the president was doing were aiding the enemy. In other words, Haldeman believed anyone who criticized the president was, in fact, a traitor. The interview made headlines around the country. And, although the public's reaction to Haldeman's statements was hardly favorable, he still took the opportunity to send Walters a note: "Thank you for making me a household name."[4]

At the same time that Walters's career woes were subsiding at *Today*, her marriage was floundering. Barbara Walters's and Lee Guber's lives had begun to separate as they each focused on their own individual careers, and Walters began to realize the two had little in common except their daughter. There was one other deciding factor:

Guber, like her father, was deeply involved in the theater, and like her father, was always certain that the next show would be a hit despite a string of failures. It was becoming too much for Walters to bear. Fortunately, she had her work to keep her busy. And an opportunity was about to arise for her to become part of history.

GOING TO CHINA

Following the Communist takeover of mainland China in 1949, the United States had had no diplomatic relations with the People's Republic of China. (The United States did, however, maintain relations with the Republic of China, also known as Taiwan, where the Nationalist government fled following its defeat in the Chinese Civil War.) In July 1971, National Security Adviser Henry Kissinger made a secret trip to visit the Communist Chinese leadership on behalf of the Nixon administration. Seven months later, in February 1972, Nixon himself went to China, becoming the first U.S. president to do so.

It was an event of historic importance. Every reporter in the nation wanted to accompany Nixon on his trip, but few were chosen. NBC sent four: its top news anchor, John

IN HER OWN WORDS

Many women have difficulties raising children. Recalling her own struggles as a mother, Barbara Walters once said:

> Motherhood is tough. If you just want a wonderful little creature to love, you can get a puppy.

Chancellor; two seasoned correspondents, Herb Kaplow and John Rich; and, much to her surprise and delight, Barbara Walters.

Three factors went into the decision to include Walters. One, the network was afraid that if Frank McGee were chosen, it would become too much of an open competition between him and John Chancellor. Two, because all the other network's reporters were white men, NBC News executives felt that Walters could contribute something different to the coverage. And three, because of the 12-hour time difference between New York and Beijing, when *The Today Show* aired live in the morning, Walters would still be appearing on the show but from Beijing, reporting live on the evening's banquets, toasts, and cultural events.

It was the first close-up view inside China that most Americans had seen in a generation. Walters covered it all. She reported on the daily activities of the president and the first lady and on the evening festivities. She visited department stores. She visited the home of a farming family. She visited an agricultural commune. She visited schools. And everywhere she went, she carried her own camera and tape recorder. It was hard yet exhilarating work, and as she said later, "I learned more about reporting than at any time since."[5]

BARBARA WALTERS STEPS UP

But when she returned from China, she would be a woman alone. Walters and Lee Guber had reached the decision that while she was overseas, he would take the opportunity to move his belongings out of their apartment and find his own place to live. Her second marriage had come to an end.

Receiving minimal child support for Jacqueline, Walters got through the pain of her failed marriage by doing what she did best: work. When news stories happened, when the

In February 1972, Barbara Walters *(right)* arrived in Beijing, China, during President Richard M. Nixon's famous visit to the communist nation. The visit would not only formally open relations between the United States and China, but would also greatly aid Walters's career.

rich, famous, and powerful had stories to tell, she was there. Her career went into a new form of overdrive.

Shortly thereafter, Walters made her first visit to the Middle East, where she got a rare interview with the Israeli defense minister, Moshe Dayan. The two became friends, and Walters took the opportunity to reconnect to her Jewish roots by visiting the sacred sites in the ancient city of Jerusalem. She spent much of the summer of 1973 in Washington, D.C., covering the hearings held by the U.S. Senate investigating President Nixon's involvement in the cover-up of the break-in at the Democratic National Committee's headquarters at the Watergate office complex. And of course, there were always celebrities to interview, which allowed her to continue to cover both hard news and entertainment.

Despite her success, McGee's feelings about Walters had not changed and tensions continued to mount on the set of *The Today Show*. In her autobiography, Walters discussed the fact that, in contrast to the time when Hugh Downs was host, she and McGee never had a meal together and never had a personal conversation. She continued to try, sending him a present for his birthday and a card at Christmas, but there was no acknowledgement from him, not even a thank you.

But even without McGee's acknowledgement, NBC brass recognized Walters's contributions. In September 1973, she signed a new contract, giving her a sizable raise. Despite her years on the show, she was still just a reporter and was not given a title that matched her responsibilities. There was, however, a clause added to her new contract that would make it possible for Walters to become the show's cohost, but only if the unthinkable were to occur. But, as often happens, the unthinkable does sometimes happen. Walters reminisced about the chain of events for the book *The Today Show: An Anecdotal History*:

> In 1974, Frank McGee had cancer. We all knew it, although he hadn't said anything. . . . When Frank died, I was on vacation and immediately flew home. NBC announced they were going to look for another host. Remember, I had now been on the program for eleven years. Obviously I had a contract. In it it stated that if Frank McGee left, voluntarily or otherwise, I would be co-host. Frank McGee was a young man, and NBC never thought they would have to honor the clause, but when Frank died, they were forced to make me co-host. Ever since then, anyone who has

come in has automatically become co-host on every morning show. And that's how it happened.[6]

Five days after Frank McGee died on April 17, 1974, NBC issued the following press release:

> Barbara Walters will be co-host of the NBC Television Network's *Today* program from now on, Donald Meaney, Vice-President, Television News Programming announced today. This is the first time the program has had a co-host, and *Today* is now the only TV network news or public affairs program to have a female co-host.[7]

Once again, Barbara Walters had made television history.

Three months later, Jim Hartz, a popular local anchor, was hired to replace McGee. It was obvious to all, however, that Barbara Walters was now the show's major draw. A 1974 *Newsweek* cover story named her "Star of the Morning." The following year, in 1975, she received the National Association of Program Executives Award of the Year, won her first Emmy for Outstanding Host in a Talk, Service, or Variety Series, and was named Broadcaster of the Year by the International Radio and Television Society. It was no wonder that that same year, *Time* named her one of the 100 most influential people in America.

She earned her accolades because she kept getting the interviews that mattered. She encouraged President Anwar Sadat of Egypt to grant her an interview by writing a note to the Egyptian ambassador, which read in part:

> Americans don't know President Sadat at all, and, as a result, they fear him and they fear your country. If your President is considering doing any interviews, he would have no better forum than the *Today* show.

Please ask him if I can come to Cairo to speak with him. Let me introduce him to the American people.[8]

Despite the fact that Sadat had never given an interview to the American press, she was invited to Cairo to meet with him three weeks later. If Sadat liked her, he would agree to the interview. It turned out, however, that it was not the president's approval she really needed. Instead, Walters spent one hour meeting with Sadat's wife, Jehan. The two hit it off, becoming friends. Walters got the interview, which made headlines and appeared on both the *Today* show and on evening news programs.

At this point in her career, Walters was at the top of her game. As contract negotiations with NBC began in the spring of 1976, no one considered the possibility that she might leave the network that had made her a star. Yet those negotiations would shake the world of network news to its core and bring Walters's career to the point where she thought it was all over.

The One-Million-Dollar Woman

While watching a tennis match being played in West-chester, New York, Fred Pierce, president of the ABC Television Network, passed a matchbook cover to Lou Weiss, Barbara Walters's representative and the head of the television department at the powerful William Morris Agency. "Five years?" Pierce wrote on the matchbook. "For five million."[1]

It was an astonishing amount of money for that era. To entice Barbara Walters to leave NBC, her professional home for more than 15 years, ABC was offering her $1 million a year—$500,000 to be paid by ABC's entertainment division for her to do four one-hour specials a year, and another $500,000 to be paid by ABC's news division for her to coanchor the *ABC Evening News* alongside veteran newsman Harry Reasoner. It was an exciting, intriguing, and frightening offer.

Money, at least according to Walters herself, was not the issue. She was making nearly that much at NBC. What was enticing to her about the offer was the opportunity to score another historic first. As long as there had been television news, it was believed that delivering the news about serious subjects such as war, politics, and natural disasters was a man's job. If she signed with ABC, she would become the first regular female coanchor on a network television news program.

The possibility of breaking another barrier for women journalists was tempting. But, as she has demonstrated time and again in her life, Walters was not an innate risk taker, having learned the dangers of taking chances from her father's career. She had a job she loved and earned more than enough money to support not only herself and her daughter, but her parents and sister as well. Why take a chance at failure?

But at the same time that ABC was making its offer, Walters was negotiating with NBC for her next contract. Problems cropped up almost immediately. NBC wanted to offer her only a three-year contract, while Walters and her agent wanted a five-year contract, feeling certain that she had earned the right to have that additional job security. In addition, Walters wanted her new NBC contract to guarantee her some degree of control over whom she would interview, what features she would do, and who, should Jim Hartz decide to leave *Today*, would be her next cohost. When NBC refused these requests and negotiations dragged on, ABC's offer became more and more attractive.

Then ABC sweetened the offer. ABC promised to expand the news program from half an hour to one hour, which would give Walters time to do the interviews that had made her famous. She was told that she would be able to help reshape the news program by making it more personal and more in-depth, in ways that had never been done before on a network news program. And there was one other thing: If Walters took ABC's offer, she would no longer have to get up long before dawn five days a week. She could have a normal life, spend more time with her daughter, and even be able to go out in the evening without having to worry about getting to bed early enough to make the next day's four-thiry A.M. alarm.

Despite the temptation, Walters instructed her agent to tell ABC thanks, but no thanks. ABC, though, would not take no for an answer and continued to pursue Walters. Then, to Walters's dismay, the news of her negotiations with ABC went public. Headlines about ABC's offer, calling her "the million-dollar news baby," became commonplace. People were shocked at the offer. Who was Barbara Walters to be earning a million dollars when legendary CBS journalist and anchor Walter Cronkite was only making half that?

What was lost in the media frenzy was the fact that Walters would be making the same money as Cronkite, approximately $500,000 per year, for coanchoring the evening news. The other $500,000 was her salary from ABC's entertainment division for hosting four "specials" a year. Once again, Walters was playing both sides of the fence, doing both hard news and entertainment, but all anyone heard during the uproar was the million-dollar offer.

Once the news went public, NBC redoubled its efforts to keep Walters, finally giving in on her demands for greater control and an extended contract. As Walters spent weeks coming to her decision, the media firestorm continued to grow. Her agent, Lee Stevens, urged her to take the ABC offer: "What an event it will be. You'll be making broadcast history. You'll be changing the world for other female journalists."[2] That got to her. The decision, she realized, was no longer just about her. It was about the role of all women in broadcasting. On April 22, 1976, she accepted ABC's offer.

Barbara Walters, television's first woman to anchor an evening news program, talks with her cohost, Harry Reasoner, in the ABC network newsroom as she prepares for her debut on October 4, 1976. Her tenure on the program would prove to be one of the most difficult periods of her career.

THE REACTION

News of the deal drew harsh criticism from other journalists and the public. A reporter for the *New Republic* quoted Walter Cronkite as describing "the sickening sensation that we were all going under, that all of our efforts to hold television news aloof from show business had failed."[3] The *New York Times* ran a story with the headline "What Makes Barbara Walters Worth a Million?"[4] And Richard Salant, the president of CBS News, complained about the blurring of the line between entertainment and news: "Is Barbara a journalist or is she Cher?"[5]

Of course, Walters had her defenders as well. Was she being attacked, many asked, simply because she was a woman breaking a barrier? Ellen Goodman, in the *Washington Post*, wrote: "There is, in my paranoid little mind, a vague suspicion that the controversy wouldn't have raged as far and deep if Ms. Walters had been Mr. Walters."[6]

As for her soon-to-be coanchor Harry Reasoner, early rumors suggested he was not in favor of Walters joining his broadcast. Initial reports indicated that he had threatened to quit if Walters came to ABC, but he later told the *New York Times*, "I am trying to keep an open mind about it."[7] At the same time though, he told *Newsweek*: "I was with her on Nixon's China trip, but I never actually saw her work. All I know about her from that trip is that she rides a bus well."[8] The signs were not good for the two coanchors to have a warm working relationship.

Faced with a continuous barrage of criticism, Walters began to regret her decision, especially after learning that ABC had decided not to expand the news program from 30 minutes to an hour. But the die was cast. Walters, who had always felt a degree of insecurity when it came to work, now had the additional pressure of having to succeed while the world watched. She would have to prove that a woman could coanchor the news and that ABC had not made a mistake by hiring her.

To make matters worse, not only was Walters being attacked from all sides, she was being made fun of as well on NBC's popular late-night sketch comedy program, *Saturday Night Live*. On that show, Gilda Radner, just weeks before Walters's premiere on ABC, introduced the world to her comedic portrayal of Walters, known as Baba Wawa. Radner's character made fun of Walters's difficulty pronouncing the letter *r* (it often sounded like a *w*) while adding additional pronunciation problems with the letter *l* as well.

Audiences found the caricatured portrayal screamingly funny, such as in this skit when Baba Wawa makes her goodbyes to NBC:

Hewwo! This is Bara Wawa hewe to say fawewell. This is my wast moment on NBC and I want to wemind you to wook fow me awong with Hawwy Weasoneh. . . .

I want to take this oppohtunity to apowogize to NBC. I don't wike weaving. Pwease twust me, it's not sowuh gwapes, but, rathaw, that anotheh

DID YOU KNOW?

Barbara Walters is not the only woman to jump into the previously all-male domain of network news anchors. From 1993 to 1995, Connie Chung coanchored *The CBS Evening News* along with Dan Rather, but that, too, was an unsuccessful pairing. In 2006, Katie Couric left her position as cohost of *Today* and seized the opportunity to become the first female solo host and managing editor of *The CBS Evening News*.

Like Barbara Walters before her, Couric faced criticism for both her salary and lack of experience as a journalist, despite her years of reporting hard news before joining *Today*. And, like Walters, when changes were made to the traditional news format so that Couric's talents as an interviewer could be better utilized, reaction forced the network to revert to the original "straight news" format.

Also like Walters at ABC in 1976, *The CBS Evening News* once again dropped back to third place in the ratings after an initial surge. Still, Couric has persevered, and both she and the program have received much critical praise as well as some of television's highest awards.

In late 2009, Diane Sawyer assumed the role of anchor for *ABC World News* when Charles Gibson retired. For the first time in television history, two of the three anchors for the major evening network news programs were women.

The late Gilda Radner was an enormous hit with her send-up of Barbara Walters on *Saturday Night Live*. Walters herself did not appreciate the portrayal until years later.

network wecognizes in me a gweat tawent for dewivering welevant news stories with cwystah cwahity to miwwions of Americans. It's the onwy weason I'm weaving. Weahhy.[9]

It was not until years later that Walters was able to see the humor in Radner's satirical yet affectionate take on her. At the time, however, she was in no mood to laugh.

The week before her premiere on ABC, Walters told *Newsweek*, "If the show doesn't make it, I'm finished. But if it does make it . . . my God, how fantastic."[10] *The ABC Evening News with Harry Reasoner and Barbara Walters* premiered on October 4, 1976, featuring a taped Walters interview with Egyptian president Anwar Sadat.

The initial reviews were good. A reviewer for the *New York Times* called Walters a "thorough professional, a remarkable woman who has risen to the top in what was once almost exclusively a man's world."[11] Early ratings were good as well. It seemed that the gamble was going to pay off.

But after the initial novelty wore off, the ratings went back to their original low levels. *The ABC Evening News*, which had been stuck in last place in the ratings without Barbara Walters, was once again in last place with her. Walters began to feel the pressure of the show's low ratings, pressure that was only compounded by the ever-increasing tension between her and her coanchor, Harry Reasoner.

Perhaps if the ratings had improved, Reasoner might have acted differently. But since the "million-dollar woman" had not lived up to the hype, he saw no cause to change his early opinion of her. He told the rest of the crew that she was a disaster and that she was bringing the show down. *New Republic* stated it clearly: "Harry Reasoner . . . seems as comfortable on camera with Walters as a governor under indictment."[12] Within months of the program's premiere, the coanchors were no longer appearing on camera together.

IN HER OWN WORDS

Despite all of the financial security and fame her job has brought her, Barbara Walters believes:

> [T]o be valued, to know, even if only once in a while, that you can do a job well is an absolutely marvelous feeling.

Rumors began to spread that Walters was on her way out. *TV Guide* wrote an editorial suggesting that she resign. Walters was convinced at times that her career was over, but she was bolstered by letters from women, angry at what Reasoner was doing to her. She also got a telegram from someone she had never met that helped her get through the difficult months. "Don't let the bastards get you down,"[13] wrote movie legend John Wayne. But still she wondered if she had made a mistake leaving the safety and security of NBC. With the failure of the Walters/Reasoner team, what could she do to salvage her career?

Rebuilding
Her Career

With the failure of *The ABC Evening News with Harry Reasoner and Barbara Walters*, Walters was now at the lowest period of her professional life. She did, however, have one way to rehabilitate her career. Her contract with ABC had, along with the coanchor position on the evening news, also given her four prime-time specials per year. Those specials would prove to be her salvation.

The first one aired on December 14, 1976. Viewers were treated to an interview with singer and film star Barbra Streisand at her Malibu ranch; an interview with President-elect Jimmy Carter and his wife, Rosalynn, at their home in Plains, Georgia; and, because the show was short one interviewee, a tour of Barbara Walters's own New York City apartment. With its mixture of entertainment and politics, it laid the groundwork for all the specials that would follow.

If Walters thought the show would improve her journalistic reputation, she was mistaken. Many of her colleagues expressed their dismay at the program, particularly on her interview with Jimmy Carter. In their eyes, it was bad enough that she engaged the Carters in a discussion of their sleeping arrangements. But to top it off, at the end of the interview, Walters asked Carter to "be wise with us. . . . Be good to us."[1]

Journalists were aghast. Morley Safer, famous for his years on *60 Minutes*, said:

> The interview with Governor Carter is really what ended Ms. Walters' brief career as a journalist and placed her firmly in the ranks of . . . what? The Merv Griffins and Johnny Carsons? What right does any reporter have to issue such a benediction? . . . It is as if Mr. Carter had just become Louis XIV and without Pope Barbara's admonition, he might be dumb with us and mean to us.[2]

Years later, Walters explained her reasons for saying what she did to the president-elect:

> That was the first special I did for ABC, at the height of the brouhaha over my salary. I wanted those specials to be different from news, to have a human quality. . . . At the end of the interview [Carter] talked about what it meant to have been elected and what he hoped to do for the country; it was very moving. So I said, "Be wise, be kind." If I had to do it all over again, I probably would edit that

out because it caused so much negative comment. But—well, what did I do that was so terrible?[3]

Despite the criticism, that first Barbara Walters special was a smashing success. With a viewing audience of more than 15 million people, it soundly beat the competing shows on the other two major networks, CBS and NBC. With its mixture of pop culture and politics, it was like nothing audiences had seen. *Entertainment Weekly* wrote, "Barbara Walters had to prove she was worth a

DID YOU KNOW?

Even Barbara Walters sometimes fails to get an interview she wants. In March 1979, Walters was shuttling back and forth between Israel and Egypt, as President Jimmy Carter was attempting to finalize a peace agreement between these two nations. While Walters was interviewing Prime Minister Menachem Begin of Israel at his home in Jerusalem, he received a telephone call from Carter and indicated to Walters that the news from Cairo, Egypt, was good. She immediately flew to Cairo via Cyprus (there were no direct flights between the two countries) and at 11:00 P.M. went directly to Egyptian president Anwar Sadat's residence in Giza.

Walters tried to persuade a security guard to take a note to Sadat telling him that she wanted just a few words from him, but to no avail. In desperation, she and her crew began throwing pebbles at Sadat's windows, hoping to get his attention. She was lucky she was not arrested for doing so, but instead, another security guard took pity on her and passed her note on to Sadat. And while he declined to meet with her, he did say in a note that he would be happy to meet with her when he traveled to Washington, D.C., to sign the final peace treaty.

million dollars, and on the night of December 14, 1976, she did."[4]

Because of the success of the first special, Walters found it easier to get guests who normally did not appear on television to sit down with her to be interviewed. Her second special featured, along with actress Elizabeth Taylor and Representative Barbara Jordan of Texas, a news-making interview with the shah of Iran and his wife, Empress Farah.

During the interview, the shah of Iran, despite having given women in his country many rights they had not previously had, expressed his belief in the inferiority of women, responded to Walters's question about women not having the same intelligence as men by answering, "Not so far. Maybe you will become in the future."[5] Walters pressed him on this point, noting that he had made his wife the regent of his country, meaning that if he should die before his son was of age, that she would become the nation's leader. Did that mean, she asked, that his wife could govern as well as a man? He responded: "I prefer not to answer that."[6]

All the while his wife was sitting besides him, her eyes wet with tears. Walters asked her how it felt to hear her husband say those things. The empress turned to him and quietly said: "I don't think you really believe that."[7] Once again, Walters's ability to get the rich and famous to reveal themselves in unexpectedly human ways have made her interview a must-see event.

Of course, she used her skills as an interviewer not just with political and world leaders, but with celebrities from the worlds of music, film, and television as well. One interview that got particular notice was with film and music legend Bing Crosby. Walters asked Crosby, then 74, a series of questions about his religious and moral beliefs that culminated in the following exchange:

Walters: Suppose one of your sons came home and said, "Dad, I've got this girl and do you mind if we share a room here in the house?"

Crosby: In OUR house? No chance!

Walters: It happens in other families.

Crosby: Well, it wouldn't happen in MY family. If any one of them did that I wouldn't speak to them ever again.

Walters: Ever again?

Crosby: Ever again.[8]

Such questioning is typical of her interviews. Walters is never rude, and she does not push too hard. Instead, while asking the questions that she feels her audience wants answered, she gently pushes her guest with charm and civility in a way that gets the guests to answer the question without feeling bullied into doing so.

Although the specials had resuscitated her career, she now had an important ally in her corner as well. In May 1977, Roone Arledge was made president of ABC News and moved quickly to repair the damage done by *The ABC Evening News with Harry Reasoner and Barbara*

DID YOU KNOW?

Barbara Walters is not the only television journalist who did celebrity interviews. Edward R. Murrow, one of the most respected journalists in radio and television history, hosted *Person to Person*, a 1950s television program in which he interviewed celebrities in their own homes while sitting in his studio in New York. Yet, unlike Barbara Walters's case, Murrow's credentials as a serious journalist were already well established and never in question.

Walters. Arledge released Reasoner from his contract, blaming him for the newscast's low ratings. He also publicly praised Walters in the *New York Times*, calling her "a professional journalist. . . . She's a great asset who has been mishandled."[9]

Nearly 30 years later, Walters reflected on what had happened to her during her time as coanchor on the evening news:

> Perhaps my experience was the price of being first, and in a very different time. Back in 1976 you could freely attack a woman for wanting to attempt to do a so-called man's job, especially in the holier-than-thou men-only news departments. Many people still believed that women were supposed to know their place—and stay in it. There were few women in front of the camera and fewer still in any executive position. Today, that same attitude would not only be politically incorrect, but the backlash would be enormous.[10]

By July 1978, *The ABC Evening News with Harry Reasoner and Barbara Walters* was no more. In its place was *World News Tonight*, with not two but three anchors: Frank Reynolds reporting from New York; Max Robinson, the first African-American news anchor, reporting from Chicago; and Peter Jennings from London. Harry Reasoner returned to CBS, where he became a regular on *60 Minutes* and, in time, apologized to and even became friendly with his old coanchor Barbara Walters.

And as for Walters herself, she escaped from the evening news debacle to become one of the network's biggest stars, getting interviews that no one else was able to. In fact, she became as well known as the famous men and women she was interviewing. Her next special, however, featured an exclusive interview with one of the best-known names in the world and became one of her most notable assignments.

FIDEL CASTRO

In 1977, after two years of effort and countless letters written to both the Cuban Mission at the United Nations as well as to the Cuban delegation in the Czech Embassy in Washington (then as now, the United States does not have diplomatic relations with Cuba), Walters got her man. President Fidel Castro of Cuba agreed to sit down for an interview with her in his native country. It was the first television interview he had granted in more than 16 years.

The special made for riveting television. Viewers witnessed Fidel Castro taking American journalist Barbara Walters on a speeding boat ride across the Bay of Pigs, the site of a failed U.S. invasion of Cuba to drive Castro from power in 1962. They saw Castro driving Walters in a jeep, one hand on the wheel, the other gesturing with a cigar, through the Sierra Maestra, the same mountains that had been the base of his revolutionary army before it came to power in 1959. Viewers also got to witness Walters asking Castro questions in a sit-down interview that ranged from whether he would ever shave off his beard to the exact number of political prisoners being held in Cuban prisons and his views on freedom of the press. But what viewers did not get to see was the entire interview.

Because Fidel Castro is a man who likes to talk and Barbara Walters is a woman who likes to ask questions, the actual interview took more than five hours to complete, after which Castro himself made grilled cheese sandwiches for Walters and her crew. Later, Castro wrote Walters a note, which translates, "For Barbara as a remembrance of

Fidel Castro responds to a question from Barbara Walters during a news conference granted to members of the U.S. press covering Senator George McGovern's trip to Havana, Cuba, on May 7, 1975. Her exhaustive interview with the Cuban leader two years later would be considered among the highlights of her career.

the most difficult interview that I have had in all the days of my life."[11]

After that triumph, though, came tragedy. Lou Walters, 81 years old and frail, died on August 15, 1977. He had been in ill health for some time, and while death is always difficult, the family had had time to prepare themselves for its eventuality. Walters arranged for obituaries to run in all the major papers, including *Variety*, the entertainment news magazine. In the glowing description of his life was the line,

"He believed in full lighting."[12] As Walters has said, "What better epitaph for a showman?"[13]

But despite her sorrow at her father's death, Walters continued to work. She would come to remember it as the most meaningful time in her professional life.

DOING THE MIDDLE EAST SHUFFLE

A month after her father's death, Walters flew to Beirut, Lebanon, for an exclusive interview with Yasser Arafat, the head of the Palestine Liberation Organization. The interview did not go well, for despite Walters's prodding, Arafat refused to answer the simple question of whether he believed the state of Israel had the right to exist. Walters left Beirut convinced that the possibility of peace in the Middle East seemed hopeless.

Several months later, in November 1977, Walters was in Kansas City interviewing country singer Dolly Parton for an upcoming special when she learned that Anwar Sadat had announced during an interview with CBS anchor Walter Cronkite that he would be willing to go to Jerusalem in search of peace. If he went, it would be the first time any Arab leader had visited the state of Israel.

The Israeli prime minister, Menachem Begin, quickly responded with an invitation to Sadat to speak directly to the nation's legislative body, the Knesset. Walter Cronkite had scored an impressive journalistic coup, but with the information now out in the open, the top journalists from the three major networks were racing to the Middle East.

As it turned out, ABC's Peter Jennings had had the opportunity to break the news himself, when Sadat told him off-camera that he would be willing to go to Jerusalem—but Jennings did not have a camera crew with him at the time, so he could not get Sadat's statement on tape. As ABC's chief foreign correspondent, Jennings faced additional dis-appointment when, instead of selecting him to cover Sadat's trip to Jerusalem, network executives gave Barbara Walters the plum assignment.

Why had Walters been given the assignment instead of Jennings, who had spent years covering the Middle East? The answer is simple. Over the years, Walters had established personal relationships with both Sadat and Begin, relationships that could come in handy when it came time to get an interview. (Unsurprisingly, Jennings was angry with Walters for years. She did not blame him for being angry, but as she admits, she did not turn down the assignment.)

Walters arrived in the Israeli city of Tel Aviv on November 18 to interview the chief of staff of the Israel Defense Forces, Moshe Dayan, when the word came that the chase for an interview with Sadat was on. CBS's Walter Cronkite was not in Israel, but in Cairo and had a seat on Sadat's plane to Tel Aviv. John Chancellor, anchor of *NBC Nightly News*, was going to be on the same plane. For her to have any chance of speaking with Sadat, Walters would have to be on that same plane.

That, however, was easier said than done. Technically, Israel and Egypt were in a state of war: Not only were there no flights between the two countries, there were not even direct phone lines. In desperation, Walters went through her phone book, filled with important contacts, and called, not even thinking about the time, Egypt's ambassador to the United States, Ashraf Ghorbal, at his home in Washington. Please, she begged him, she had to get a seat on that plane. What could he do to help?

Ghorbal called back two hours later to tell her that he had gotten her a seat on the plane. Now all she had to do was get to Cairo. Hearing about a French jet that had been chartered by CBS to fly its satellite equipment from Paris to Tel Aviv, she paid the French pilots to fly her to Egypt. The plane would stop briefly in Cyprus (no direct flights between Egypt and Israel were allowed) before landing in Cairo.

But, due to the historic event about to take place, the plane did not stop in Cyprus, as had been planned, and instead flew directly to Cairo, allowing Walters just enough time to make the plane. Cronkite later recalled looking out the window of the plane to see Walters running across the tarmac, gesturing for the plane to wait for her. Unsurprisingly, neither Cronkite nor Chancellor was happy about seeing their rival catch up with them. "I couldn't have been unhappier,"[14] Cronkite said later.

It turned out that he was soon going to be even unhappier. Unable to speak to Sadat privately on the plane to Tel Aviv, Walters passed a note to one of his aides with the question, "Mr. President, would you agree to do an interview with me after you speak at the Knesset?"[15]

To make things even easier for him, she had put four boxes on the bottom of the page: "Yes;" "No;" "Alone"; "With PM Begin." Just before exiting the plane, an aide to Sadat returned the note with the boxes "Yes" and "Alone" checked. It would have been better, she thought, if she could have gotten an interview with Sadat and Begin together, but once again, she had gotten the interview she wanted.

After arriving in Tel Aviv, where Sadat was welcomed to Israel by Begin, Golda Meir (the former Israeli prime minister), and Moshe Dayan, Walters drove to Jerusalem, where she had arranged to interview Begin. After their interview was over, Begin had a surprise for her.

On their drive from the airport in Tel Aviv to Jerusalem, Begin had asked Sadat, "For the sake of our friend Barbara, would you do the interview tomorrow with me together?"[16] Sadat readily agreed. After Sadat's historic address at the Knesset, Walters sat down to do the first joint interview with the two leaders, bringing them together before the

One of Barbara Walters's great "gets"—a sit-down interview with Prime Minister Menachem Begin of Israel (*center*) and President Anwar Sadat (*left*) of Egypt in Jerusalem, at the time when the two leaders were discussing a formal peace treaty between their two nations.

entire world to discuss the possibility for peace between their nations.

After insisting that they be given equal access, both Cronkite and Chancellor were granted joint interviews. Their interviews, however, were conducted after Walters's and broadcast later, and it is her interview that is remembered. For their work in promoting peace in the Middle East, Walters, Cronkite, and Chancellor received the $10,000 Hubert H. Humphrey Freedom Prize by the B'nai B'rith Anti-Defamation League.

Perhaps more importantly, with that interview, Walters had reestablished her own status in the news division of ABC. In her autobiography, she recalled:

> The back-to-back interviews with Castro and Arafat, followed by the interview with Sadat and Begin, had put me back on the map as a serious journalist. It didn't hurt that I'd gone head-to-head with Chancellor and Cronkite . . . and, you should excuse the expression, beaten the pants off them. From then on I was more or less accepted as a member of the old boy's club.[17]

She had successfully resuscitated her career from the debacle of *The ABC Evening News with Harry Reasoner and Barbara Walters*. Now firmly reestablished as one of ABC's most important journalists and interviewers, she was in a position to call her own shots and do the kind of work she wanted to do.

The Art of the Interview

As her contract with ABC was coming to an end in 1981, Walters was faced with a major decision. Should she stay with the network where, after a rocky beginning, her career was now flourishing? Or should she take an offer from CBS to join what was then the top-rated show on television, *60 Minutes*?

Still averse to risk taking and knowing she had the president of ABC News strongly in her corner, Walters decided not to move to CBS. She signed a five-year contract with ABC that guaranteed her four prime-time specials a year, occasional hard-news assignments, and the opportunity to fill in for David Hartman on *Good Morning America* and for Ted Koppel on *Nightline* whenever either host was unavailable. Plus, there was an additional assignment, one that reunited her with her old *Today* show host, Hugh Downs.

The program was *20/20*, ABC's own news magazine, which was created in response to the overwhelming popularity of *60 Minutes*. Because it had premiered in 1978 to lukewarm reviews, Roone Arledge had turned to Walters to ask her if she would be interested in being the show's anchor. But, having just come off of her disastrous stint as coanchor of the evening news, she politely declined the offer. Arledge then turned to Hugh Downs, who was in semiretirement, and asked him to take over the show. With Downs in the anchor chair, the ratings of the revamped *20/20* immediately improved. For the next three years, Walters contributed pieces to the show, but the question of her anchoring seemed to have been taken off the table. But Arledge was not ready to give up. If the program was doing well with Hugh Downs, would it not do even better with Walters serving as his cohost?

This time, Walters agreed to do so. While she had plenty of work at ABC, she did not have a steady "home" in the network's news division. *20/20* would become her regular base, where viewers could see her every week at a regular time, and she could do the program without the pressure of hosting it by herself. And to top it off, she would be working again with her old friend Hugh Downs, a man for whom she had the utmost affection and respect.

Much to her surprise, however, Downs was opposed to her becoming his coanchor. It was nothing against her personally; he was simply against the idea of anyone becoming coanchor and was not willing to share the show's success. But Arledge insisted, and while Downs made it clear to Walters his feelings on the subject, he now had a coanchor.

Downs wanted top billing, however, and got it. Walters would do the high-profile interviews she was known for, while Downs would concentrate on the more low-key and entertaining features (such as swimming with sharks) that he was known for. Despite his initial misgivings, he knew they worked well together. As the show's ratings grew even higher, he was forced to admit to Walters, "I don't know when I've been happier to have been wrong."[1]

Indeed, the two often seemed to make up a mutual admiration society. Walters told an interviewer for *Good Housekeeping* in 1992, "If Hugh had not fought for my opportunity to appear regularly on *Today*, I would not have happened in this business."[2] For his part, Downs insists that her success is entirely due to her hard work and talent. "In truth, she discovered herself," he told *Good Housekeeping*. "With her talents, she would eventually have happened without me."[3]

POPULAR INTERVIEWER

Barbara Walters was now the most popular interviewer on television. Everybody who was anybody sat down with her to share their story, share their lives, and, if viewers were lucky, to have a good cry in front of the cameras. (Walters became famous for asking such probing personal questions that her guests often ended up in tears by the end of the interview.)

While her "celebrity" interviews were generally saved for her *Barbara Walters Specials*, her *20/20* interviews tended to focus on everyday people who suddenly found themselves the center of the public's attention, particularly those involved in controversy or accused of criminal activities.

She interviewed Jean Harris, the headmistress of the elite Madeira School for girls, who was accused of murdering her lover, the "Scarsdale diet" doctor Herman Tarnower. She interviewed Danish socialite Claus von Bulow, accused of poisoning his wife, Sunny. She interviewed Donna Rice, a young woman whose affair with Senator Gary Hart had doomed his chance at the Democratic nomination for the presidency. She interviewed Jack Kevorkian, the infamous "assisted suicide" doctor.

One Walters interview that gained widespread attention was with heavyweight boxing champion Mike Tyson and his wife, actress Robin Givens. For months, rumors had been circulating that the couple's marriage was in trouble and that Tyson was suffering from depression and had been physically abusing his wife. The couple attempted to use the interview to clear the air, but the results were just the opposite. Much to the surprise of Walters and viewers, Givens spoke bitterly about Tyson's anger and temper, describing their marriage as "worse than anything I could possibly imagine."[4] Their marriage ended shortly thereafter in divorce, but the interview garnered huge ratings and proved once again that sitting down for an interview with Barbara Walters could be a dangerous thing to do.

Of course, she interviewed other people besides those known solely for unfortunate behavior. She has, for example, sat down to talk with every U.S. president (and first lady) since Richard Nixon. But one of those White House interviews raised an important journalistic problem. Which is more important—the public's right to know or a person's right to privacy?

The interview was with First Lady Betty Ford, the wife of President Gerald Ford. As Mrs. Ford accompanied Walters on a tour of the living quarters of the White House, it became clear that the first lady, who was slurring her words and was having difficulty putting a sentence together, was under the influence of either alcohol or drugs. Then later, during the sit-down portion of the interview, the first lady had a glass of a pale liquid by her side. Even when President Ford asked her if she *had* to have the drink, she kept it.

Walters was faced with a decision. Should she show the portion of the interview that showed Mrs. Ford to be obviously inebriated? Or should she edit that portion out and leave the Ford family to deal in private with what was obviously a difficult situation? It was her interview; it was up to her to determine what stayed and what should be cut out.

In her autobiography, Walters wrote that while the decision may have made her a lousy reporter, she decided to omit the first lady's slurred voice. Instead, while she kept the visuals of Mrs. Ford showing her around the family's quarters in the White House, Walters recorded a voice-over description of what the viewer was seeing. Walters felt that if Mrs. Ford had a drinking problem, she did not want to be the one to make it public. Two years after this interview, the Ford family staged an intervention with Mrs. Ford, who was forced to confront her addiction to alcohol as well as painkillers that had been prescribed years earlier for a pinched nerve. In 1982, Betty Ford established the Betty Ford Center in Mirage, California, for the treatment of chemical dependency.

MEETING THE WORLD

In addition to interviewing U.S. presidents, Walters has interviewed more than 30 world leaders over the course of her career. One particular noteworthy interview was the one she conducted with Prime Minister Margaret Thatcher, the "Iron Lady" of British politics, who took Walters on a tour of the prime minister's official living quarters at 10 Downing Street in London, England. Thatcher explained to Walters how her father had taught her the meaning of leadership:

> You never just follow the crowd for the sake of following the crowd because you don't like to stand out. You make up your own mind what is right. And then you try to persuade other people to follow you. It was quite a tough thing for a child, but it was very,

very firm in my father's upbringing. It has stood me in very good stead since.[5]

She also interviewed Jean-Claude Duvalier, the recently deposed dictator of Haiti known as "Baby Doc," and his wife, Michèle, known as the "Dragon Lady." The two had been accused by Haiti's new government of stealing up to $400 million from the developing nation's treasury, and the Duvaliers wanted to use the opportunity to appear on television to deny those charges.

Unfortunately, the Duvaliers decided to do the interview at their villa located in the south of France, a location that seemed to prove that those charges were, indeed, true. Their case was not helped by the fact that Mrs. Duvalier appeared for the interview wearing a designer suit, diamond earrings, a diamond ring, and a diamond brooch, while denying that she had a special room in her palace in Haiti just to store her furs since, as she said, the entire palace was air-conditioned.

When Walters asked her if she knew or even cared that most people in Haiti were not only living without air-conditioning, but without electricity or even running water, Mrs. Duvalier seemed perplexed that the question was being asked. As the Duvaliers made themselves look worse and worse, Walters wondered why they had agreed to the interview in the first place. But if the Duvaliers did not understand what the interview revealed about them, viewers did. For months afterward, Haitians would come up to Barbara Walters on the street and thank her for exposing their former leaders for what they were.

DIFFICULTIES

As successful as her professional life was at this time, Walters's personal life was suffering in the late 1980s and early 1990s. In 1985, just before giving a speech in Milwaukee,

Barbara Walters talks with exiled Haitian dictator Jean-Claude Duvalier at his villa in Grasse, France, on June 12, 1986. The interview seemed to prove that the corruption charges pertaining to Duvalier and his wife were in fact true.

she received a phone call from her sister Jacqueline's doctor, informing her that Jacqueline had died. Walters, grief-stricken, wiped the tears from her eyes and went on to make the speech. How could she go through with it? Walters asked herself a similar question in her autobiography: "What does that say about me? I don't know. Maybe I don't want to know. I just did my job, which seems to be what I do no matter what the circumstance. Maybe it's the way I cope."[6]

On May 10, 1986, she married Merv Adelson, the chairman of Lorimar Productions. But after a brief honeymoon, the hardworking couple returned to their separate lives:

Walters to New York City and Adelson to Los Angeles. Unable to stand the strain of their bicoastal lifestyle, the marriage, Walters's third, ended in divorce in 1992.

Then, in June 1988, Walters's 91-year-old mother died after a long and difficult life. Walters was not with her mother at the time of her death, but was instead celebrating her daughter's twentieth birthday. To this day, Walters feels guilty that she was not with her mother and dreams about her all the time.

During this period, there were also difficulties at work. In November 1986, news of the Iran-Contra arms deal first surfaced, in which senior officials in the Reagan administration secretly and without congressional assent agreed to sell arms to Iran in order to secure the release of U.S. hostages and to fund Nicaraguan anticommunist rebels, or contras. Walters had interviewed two men with connections in the Iran-Contra affair: a Saudi Arabian businessman, Adnan Khashoggi, and an Iranian arms dealer, Manucher Ghorbanifar. After completing their interview, Ghorbanifar asked Walters to deliver some documents to President Ronald Reagan that were reported to contain confidential information about payments being made to Iranian officials. Walters agreed, hoping that the documents might help to speed the release of American hostages being held in Lebanon.

It was a huge mistake. By every rule of journalism, reporters are not supposed to become involved in the story themselves and are not supposed to act as messengers. Walters's initial problem, however, was getting the documents to the president. She contacted a friend, Jerry Zipkin, who was also friends with Nancy Reagan, the president's wife. After hearing from Zipkin that Walters needed to talk to her, Mrs. Reagan called Walters, who told her a bit of what was happening. The first lady then put the president on the line, who told Walters how best to get the documents to him.

Walters then told her bosses at ABC what had happened and gave them a copy of the memo she had given the White House about Ghorbanifar, explaining her reasons for doing what she did—that if she did not, Ghorbanifar's life would be in danger, and there was the possibility that if she did pass the documents on, American hostages would be released. That night, ABC reported on what had happened without mentioning Ghorbanifar's name or Walters's role in the story.

It would probably have ended there if the *Wall Street Journal* had not picked up the story in March 1987, with a story headlined: "Iran Arms Dealer Used Barbara Walters to Secretly Pass on a Message to Reagan."[7] With this, Walters came under fire from both the public and the press. ABC itself felt obliged to reprimand Walters publicly for her actions, issuing the following statement to the press:

> Barbara Walters' transmission of her information to the president was in violation of a literal interpretation of news policy. ABC News policy expressly limits journalistic cooperation with government agencies unless threats to human life are involved. Miss Walters believed that to be the case.[8]

Walters was disappointed that the network had reprimanded her in public because she believed that she was saving lives. But soon enough the smoke cleared, and Walters went on doing what she did best—reporting the news and interviewing people who made the news.

But out of all the interviews she has ever done, of all the world leaders, of all the celebrities, of all the rich and famous (and infamous), the one that got the most attention, made the biggest headlines, and grabbed the biggest ratings was the one she conducted with a 26-year-old former White House intern named Monica Lewinsky, who had been involved in a sexual relationship with President Bill Clinton. What is interesting about this story is not so much what Lewinsky did; it is what Barbara Walters had to do to get the interview before anyone else. It was, as she has said, the biggest "get" of her career.

As we will learn, even Barbara Walters has to make an extraordinary effort to get an interview that everybody else is also trying to get.

CHASING MONICA

The story first made headlines on January 21, 1998. In brief, Lewinsky had confided to a friend, Linda Tripp, about her intimate relationship with Clinton. Tripp, without her friend's knowledge, then passed the information on to the U.S. Office of the Independent Counsel, which was investigating other issues relating to the conduct of the president and the first lady, Hillary Rodham Clinton.

Much to Lewinsky's surprise and dismay, while meeting Tripp for lunch in January 1998, she found herself being questioned by two FBI agents, who threatened her with imprisonment if she did not reveal everything about her relationship with the president. After 12 hours of questioning, Lewinsky was allowed to contact her mother and an attorney.

When the story broke, Lewinsky went from obscurity to being one of the best-known names in the world. (In 1998 alone, her name was mentioned in the media more than 100,000 times.) Walters, like every other journalist in the country, wanted nothing more than to get the first interview with Lewinsky. It would, however, be far easier said than done.

Instead of going directly to Lewinsky, Walters decided to go through Lewinsky's attorney, William Ginsburg. The problem was that Ginsburg was spending so much time on television being interviewed himself that he was nearly impossible to reach. One of Walters's producers, Katie Thomson, found a solution to that problem. Seeing him interviewed live on television, Thomson contacted a security guard at that station and asked him to put Ginsburg on the phone as he was leaving.

The arrangements made, Walters and Thomson flew to Washington, D.C., for a secret meeting with Ginsburg. Because Ginsburg was a fan of Walters, he told her, off the record, that while he could not say much, he could state that there was a relationship between Lewinsky and the president. Walters needed Ginsburg in order to get to Lewinsky, so she kept the secret and waited patiently for the next steps to unfold. Since Lewinsky remained in hiding from the press, Walters knew Ginsburg was the key to getting the interview. She did everything she could to put him at ease and get him on her side, even inviting him to go with her to a gala party celebrating *Time*'s seventy-fifth anniversary.

Of course, Walters was not the only reporter courting Ginsburg. Mike Wallace of *60 Minutes* invited him to dinner. Other reporters were offering theater tickets, tickets to sporting events, and even a meeting with famed photographer Richard Avedon to Ginsburg to get the interview with Lewinsky. Walters, however, seemed to have the inside track. Her relationship with Ginsburg had developed to the point that in April 1998, she became the first reporter to have a private meeting with Lewinsky. The meeting went well, but Walters was still a long way from getting the interview. Lewinsky was still in terror of being arrested, and after six months had passed without a deal being made with the independent counsel's office, she and her family replaced Ginsburg with a new team of attorneys. Walters would have to start the courtship process all over again.

Fortunately, Walters knew two of Lewinsky's attorneys from interviews she had done with two of their previous clients. Both lawyers had been impressed with Walters's work, convinced that she had been fair. Walters was hopeful that this would help her get the Lewinsky interview as well.

Events began to move forward during the summer and fall of 1998, as Lewinsky testified, in exchange for immunity, about her relationship with Clinton, and as Clinton himself admitted publicly that he had had an inappropriate relationship with Lewinsky. Convinced that her legal problems were behind her, Lewinsky began to consider the best way for her to get her side of the story out to a public.

But there was another factor involved besides simply getting her story out—her legal fees had been enormous. She was more than a million dollars in debt. If she granted her first interview to a news division in a foreign country such as the United Kingdom, she could be paid for her story. If she granted her first interview to an American talk show or American magazine, she could also get paid for her story. But if she decided to give her first interview to an American television news department, which would give her the greatest chance to help repair her reputation, she would not be paid for her story, since policies were in place in those departments not to pay for interviews.

Lewinsky, along with her spokeswoman Judy Smith, began to meet with different journalists. It was widely reported that Rupert Murdoch was offering her $5 million for two interviews, one for his Fox network in the United States and another with a British interviewer to be broadcast worldwide. While this rumor was never confirmed, there is no question that a lot of money was being offered to Lewinsky to tell her story.

Because she worked for ABC News, Walters had no money to offer Lewinsky. But, determined to get the interview, she set up a conference call with David Westin (president of ABC News), Lewinsky's mother, Marcia Lewis, Lewinsky, and herself. Their goal? To convince Lewinsky that, although she could get a lot of money selling her story, it would be best for her to tell her story for free to Barbara Walters. Walters recalled that

> over and above the money was the matter of her future credibility. For the rest of her life, we said, her credibility should be her major concern. Somehow she would find the money to pay her legal bills. I fully believed what we were saying. Of course I wanted to do the interview, but I was not so ambitious that I didn't have a conscience.[9]

A compromise was suggested. David Westin told Lewinsky that while ABC could not pay her for the interview, it could promise to broadcast it only once, and then only in the United States and Canada. Then, after that, if Lewinsky wanted to do a paid interview for the international market, she would be able to do so, since nobody overseas would have seen the ABC interview. (Keep in mind that this was before the days of YouTube and other ways for media to be simultaneously shared worldwide.)

Lewinsky did not accept the offer right away. More meetings were held between Walters and Lewinsky's family, and between Walters and Lewinsky herself. In November 1998, Lewinsky met with Walters and her production team for lunch at Walters's apartment. Walters, who likes to keep her interview subjects fresh, attempted to cut Lewinsky off whenever she brought up something that might also come up in the interview. After much discussion and much hand-holding and encouragement by Walters, Lewinsky relented. She would do her first interview with ABC.

It had been nearly a year since the Lewinsky story broke, a year Walters had spent "cultivating contacts, consulting with representatives, meeting with members of her family,

Monica Lewinsky *(right)* poses with Barbara Walters in a publicity photograph for *20/20*, the ABC News program on which Walters interviewed Lewinsky in 1999.

and slowly gaining her trust. . . . I believed in my heart that I could do the best possible interview for her."[10]

Walters immediately set to work preparing for the interview. She read hundreds of pages of transcripts of the phone conversations between Linda Tripp and Monica Lewinsky. She read the Starr Report, an investigative account by independent counsel Kenneth Starr released on September 11, 1998. She read the grand jury testimony of the major characters in the case and read the speeches that President Clinton had given on the subject.

It was a mountain of paperwork to digest, and to Walters, it seemed that she was reading day and night for weeks on end. An initial list of 200 possible questions was gradually honed down until finally, on February 20, 1999, under tight security to keep the news from getting out, Monica Lewinsky sat down with Barbara Walters to tell her story. The interview lasted over four and half hours. The transcript was 150 pages long. Those four and half hours of talk were cut down to fit the restraints of a two-hour special, and, on March 3, 1999, the interview was finally aired on *20/20*.

Nearly 50 million people watched the show, the largest audience for any Barbara Walters interview ever aired. Indeed, so many people were watching that there were reports that the water level in some cities noticeably dropped during commercials, as large numbers of people used their bathrooms and all flushed their toilets at the same time.

Once again, through drive and determination and hard work, Walters had scooped the competition and gotten one of the biggest interviews of her career. For many people, that would have been enough, a capstone on a brilliant career. But Barbara Walters was about to make a move that returned her to her career beginnings, while at the same time introducing her to a whole new audience.

Enjoying the View

In 1987, Barbara Walters said, recalling her time on *Today*, "I was very happy. But I would never go back and do another morning show."[1] But times change, things change, and, a "never" uttered at one time can be easily and quickly forgotten years later if the time and offer are right.

It is not as if Walters did not have a busy schedule. She was still hosting *20/20*. She was still doing four of her specials a year. But ABC had a problem: The programming in its 11 A.M. time slot was in trouble, and the network wanted a replacement. Unsurprisingly, given her broadcasting history, ABC executives turned to Walters and her longtime producer, Bill Geddie, to ask if they had any ideas for a daytime program.

It turned out that she did have an idea, one that she had been toying with for some time. She told ABC's programming executives: "I've always wanted to do a show with women of different generations, background and views."[2] The network was interested enough to allow Walters to tape a pilot, but with one stipulation: In addition to producing the program, Walters would have to appear on it in order to attract the interest of advertisers. Although wary, she told executives that she would do it if she could appear on the show just two or three days a week and if she did not have to be the show's moderator.

Now Walters had just one problem: finding, as she put it, "four smart women of different ages and different personalities who could disagree without killing one another and, better still, might actually like each other."[3] Auditions were set up, and, much to the surprise of Walters and Geddie, the first group of four women they auditioned turned out to be *The View*'s first hosts. Meredith Vieira, a longtime journalist who had once been a regular on *60 Minutes*, would be the show's moderator. She would be joined by Star Jones, a former attorney and reporter for Court TV; comedian Joy Behar; and Debbie Matenopoulos, who had worked for MTV and was hired to present the "young person's" point of view.

Walters and Geddie would be coexecutive producers, and Walters's own Barwall Productions, along with the daytime division of ABC, would produce the show itself. The goal of the show was to be unrehearsed and spontaneous. To help achieve that goal, *The View* would be broadcast live, five days a week.

Premiering on August 11, 1997, the show opened, as it always does, with "Hot Topics"—an open discussion among the women of what is being discussed in the country that day. "Hot Topics" is followed by interviews with a wide variety of guests, ranging from celebrities and politicians to writers.

The first weeks of the show received mixed reviews. Critics appreciated the show's concept, as well as the contributions of the majority of the cast, with the exception of Matenopoulos, whose lack of experience they felt showed in comparison to the other women. By far, the majority of the praise went to Walters herself, with a critic for the *New York Times* writing:

> [Walters] and her production company deserve full credit for guiding this show in such a smart direction. During hot topics, it is often her voice that marks out some complicated middle ground and prevents "The View" from becoming "Crossfire for Girls." This show dares to assume that women, even those watching at home in the morning, have minds of their own.[4]

Since shortly after the program's debut in 1997, *The View* has been a huge hit for ABC and for Barbara Walters. And the show has thrived despite frequent changes on the panel. Debbie Matenopoulos, who did not work out as a cast member, was replaced in 1999 by Lisa Ling, who later became an international correspondent for *National Geographic* and for Oprah Winfrey. Elisabeth Hasselbeck, who came to the public's attention through the hit reality television show *Survivor*, replaced Ling in 2003. Hasselbeck quickly made a name for herself on the show as a young woman with outspoken conservative beliefs, making her a perfect counterpoint to the more liberal panel members.

After nine years as the show's moderator, Meredith Vieira left *The View* in 2006 to replace Katie Couric on *Today* and was replaced by Rosie O'Donnell. (Around the

From left, Meredith Vieira, Star Jones, Joy Behar, and Barbara Walters appear on the set of ABC's *The View* on June 5, 2003. Since its debut in 1997, the program has been an enormous success for Walters, who both appears on the panel and serves as an executive producer with Bill Geddie.

same time, Star Jones left the show in the midst of a contract dispute. It was decided, though, that one new cast member was enough for one year, and for the time being, she was not replaced.) The selection of Rosie O'Donnell—comedian, lesbian, and outspoken liberal—brought new life to the show. Ratings skyrocketed as viewers tuned in to watch the fireworks when O'Donnell let loose. But what had been entertaining at first began to become controversial, and after a much publicized, live on-air argument with Elisabeth Hasselbeck, O'Donnell asked to be released from her contract and left the show in 2007.

Her replacement was Academy Award–winning actress Whoopi Goldberg, who made her debut on September

4, 2007. Walters was thrilled with the choice, especially after the explosive discussions that had occurred during O'Donnell's stint as moderator. She wrote in her autobiography: "Whoopi has such wisdom along with her humor. She is mellow and at the same time contributes to the edginess the program needs. We had made the perfect choice."[5] One week later, Sherri Shepherd, a standup comedian, joined the cast. As the show entered its eleventh season, the only original members left were Joy Behar and Walters herself. But despite the changes and turmoil (or perhaps because of them), the show today is more popular than ever.

CUTTING BACK

As Barbara Walters entered her seventies, she knew it was time for her to start cutting back. On January 26, 2004, after 25 years as host, she announced she would no longer be hosting *20/20*. Why did she decide to leave?

She was still getting the interviews that everybody else wanted to get. Mariah Carey, Al Gore, and even, once again, Fidel Castro all sat down to talk to Walters. But it was becoming increasingly difficult to reach audiences with interviews of that kind. Instead, audiences seemed to be more interested in interviews with people in the news for all the wrong reasons: celebrities with personal problems, controversies, or criminal behavior. The days when Walters could find a balance between hard-news and celebrity interviews for *20/20* and her specials were coming to an end.

Her last day at work on *20/20* seemed to illustrate perfectly the direction in which television news magazines were going. Walters had two potential interviews. One was with Mary Kay Letourneau, a teacher who had become infamous for having a sexual relationship with an underage student. She had just been released from a seven-year prison term and wanted to talk about her experience. The other possible interview was with President George W. Bush, who had just received the Republican Party's nomination for reelection in 2004. As Walters recalled in her autobiography: "The president of the United States or a convicted child molester? The president? The child molester? The president? The child molester? The powers that be chose Mary Kay Letourneau. I rest my case."[6]

Despite leaving *20/20*, Walters continues to appear regularly on *The View* and still produces her specials, which have begun to move away from their celebrity-driven formats to shows on topics of particular interest to her, including *Live to Be 150*, and *Heaven: Where Is It? And How Do We Get There?* She also hosts a weekly radio show on Sirius Satellite Radio, on which she discusses important topics of the day and interviews a wide variety of noted figures, from fashion designer Oscar de la Renta to Speaker of the House Nancy Pelosi.

In 2008, she completed her autobiography, *Audition*, which was published to wide acclaim. The book became a national best seller and made headlines across the country due to the revelation that Walters had, for several years in the 1970s, carried on a secret romance with Senator Edward W. Brooke, the first African American elected to the Senate since Reconstruction. After an almost 50-year career in broadcasting, Walters was still able to make news.

She was also still able to get the interviews that mattered. For example, on November 24, 2008, Walters was sitting in her dressing room at *The View* when she received a call from ABC News. Barack Obama, who had just won an election to the White House three weeks earlier, wanted to sit down with his wife, Michelle, and do an interview with Walters the next day. Could she do it?

Of course she could. She went on, as planned, to film that day's episode of *The View*, and then taped an additional

Barbara Walters arrives in the pressroom with her Emmy for life-time achievement at the News and Documentary Emmy Awards at Lincoln Center in New York City on September 21, 2009.

program that would be broadcast during the upcoming Thanksgiving holidays. After that, she went to Sirius to do her hour-long radio show. At six o'clock that evening, she met with her producers to prepare for the interview.

One set of questions was written for the president-elect and another set for Michelle Obama, who would join her husband halfway through the show. The questions were finalized late that night, and early the next morning, Walters and her crew took an early morning flight to Chicago. At five o'clock that afternoon, Walters did the interview, which took an hour.

Walters and her crew then went back to the airport to fly back to New York, and, working late into the night and into the early morning with six tape editors and three producers, produced a finished one-hour *Barbara Walters Special*. She then made the rounds to help promote the show, appearing on *Good Morning America*, *The View*, four radio programs, five other entertainment programs, and the local news, as well as ABC's *World News Tonight* and *Nightline*. The show aired at ten o'clock that evening, and Walters was able to watch, exhausted, but proud of the work she had done.

IN HER OWN WORDS

Today, Barbara Walters is more at peace with herself than she has ever been. She believes:

> What I feel more and more is how important it is to live your life in a better way, and not to worry about it. What happens will happen.

ICON

Today, Barbara Walters is a living legend, an icon and role model for female television journalists throughout the world. The next time you watch a morning news show, the local news, the network news, or a television news magazine, notice how many women there are working as reporters and journalists. Many, if not all, owe a big thanks to Barbara Walters for being the first, for being the trail-blazer, for making it all possible.

On September 21, 2009, the Television Academy of Arts and Sciences presented Barbara Walters its Lifetime Achievement Award at the Thirtieth Annual News and Documentary Emmy Awards. The plaque presented to her read:

> A consummate interviewer, top-notch correspon-dent and broadcast journalist for over forty years: Barbara Walters has served as an inspiration for aspiring women broadcasters, and has set the stan-dard of excellence for all television journalists.[7]

Today, Walters is, in her own words, happier than she has ever been. And although she has slowed down, she shows no sign of actually stopping. It seems likely that as long as there are news stories to be reported and interest-ing, famous people to be interviewed, Barbara Walters will keep doing what she does, better than anybody else.

CHRONOLOGY

1929   Barbara Jill Walters is born on September 25 to Lou and Dena Walters.

1947   She graduates from Birch Wathen High School in New York City.

1951   Walters receives a B.A. in English from Sarah Lawrence College in New York.

1952   She works in the promotion department at WNBT and becomes the station's youngest producer the following year.

1955   Walters marries Bob Katz; hired as a staff writer for CBS News.

1956   She attracts the notice of CBS executives with her work arranging interviews with survivors of the collision between the *Stockholm* and the *Andrea Doria*.

1958   Walters divorces Bob Katz.

1961   She joins NBC's *Today* as a staff writer.

1962   Walters reports on First Lady Jacqueline Kennedy's trip to India and Pakistan.

1963   She marries Lee Guber.

1964   Walters assumes the role of *Today* reporter, the new title for the *Today* Girl.

1968   She adopts her daughter, Jacqueline.

1971   Walters assumes the position of host of *Not for Women Only*.

1974   She becomes the first female coanchor of *Today*.

1975   Walters wins her first Emmy Award for her work on *Today*.

1976	She leaves NBC for ABC and begins a one-year stint coanchoring the *ABC Evening News* with Harry Reasoner; she divorces Lee Guber.
1977	Lou Walters dies on August 15.
1978	After groundbreaking interviews with Egyptian president Anwar Sadat and Israeli prime minister Menachem Begin, Walters wins the Hubert H. Humphrey Freedom Prize from the Anti-Defamation League of B'nai B'rith.
1979	She becomes a regular contributor to *20/20*.
1980	Walters wins Emmy Awards for Best News Program Segment and Best News, and shares a third Emmy for Best News and Documentary Program for her work on *Nightline*.
1984	She is named cohost (with Hugh Downs) of *20/20*.
1985	Her older sister, Jacqueline, born intellectually impaired, dies of ovarian cancer.
1986	Walters marries Merv Adelson.
1988	Dena Walters dies in June.
1990	Walters becomes the first woman inducted into the Academy of Television Arts and Sciences Hall of Fame.
1997	She becomes executive producer and cohost of *The View*.

1999   Her interview with Monica Lewinsky attracts the largest audience of any news special in television history.

2004   Walters retires as cohost of *20/20*.

2008   She publishes her autobiography, *Audition*.

2009   Walters wins Emmy Award (along with Whoopi Goldberg, Joy Behar, Elisabeth Hasselbeck, and Sherri Shepherd) for Outstanding Talk Show Host for *The View*. Wins Lifetime Achievement Award by the Television Academy of Arts and Sciences at the Thirtieth Annual News and Documentary Emmy Awards.

2010   Walters undergoes open heart surgery in May to replace a faulty heart valve; doctors are pleased with the surgery.

NOTES

CHAPTER 1

1. Gerry Davis, *The Today Show: An Anecdotal History*. New York: Quill William Morrow, 1987, p. 16.
2. Ibid., p. 21.
3. Barbara Walters, *Audition: A Memoir*. New York: Vintage Books, 2009, p. 106.
4. The View, ABC. "Featured: Q&A with Barbara Walters." http://theview.abc.go.com/blog/qa-barbara-walters.
5. Nicholas Lemann. "I Have to Ask: How Barbara Walters Got Where She Is." *New Yorker*, May 12, 2008. http://www.newyorker.com/arts/critics/books/2008/05/12/080512crbo_books_lemann.
6. Fox News. "Barbara Walters 'On the Record.'" May 7, 2009. http://www.foxnews.com/story/0,2933,519097,00.html.
7. Henna Remstein, *Barbara Walters*. Philadelphia: Chelsea House Publishers, 1999, p. 98.

CHAPTER 2

1. Walters, *Audition*, pp. 3–4.
2. Ibid., p. 28.
3. Ibid., p. 20.
4. Ibid., p. 4.

CHAPTER 3

1. Walters, *Audition*, p. 43.
2. Ibid., p. 4.
3. Ibid., p. 43.
4. Jerry Oppenheimer, *Barbara Walters: An Unauthorized Biography*. New York: St. Martin's Press, 1990, p. 40.
5. Walters, *Audition*, p. 68.
6. Ibid., p. 70.

CHAPTER 4

1. Walters, *Audition*, p. 74.
2. Ibid., p. 75.
3. Ibid., p. 77.
4. Remstein, *Barbara Walters*, p. 44.
5. Ibid.
6. Walters, *Audition*, p. 86.
7. Remstein, *Barbara Walters*, p. 46.

CHAPTER 5

1. Walters, *Audition*, p. 110.
2. Ibid.
3. Ibid., p. 111.
4. Oppenheimer, *Barbara Walters*, p. 132.
5. Ibid.
6. Ibid.
7. Davis, *The Today Show*, p. 49.
8. Walters, *Audition*, p. 147.
9. Ibid.
10. Ibid., p. 151.
11. Ibid., p. 152.
12. Ibid., p. 157.
13. Ibid., p. 174.
14. Remstein, *Barbara Walters*, p. 60.
15. Ibid., p. 57.
16. Walters, *Audition*, p. 171.

CHAPTER 6

1. Walters, *Audition*, p. 149.
2. Ibid., p. 205.
3. Ibid.
4. Ibid., p. 208.
5. Ibid., p. 227.
6. Davis, *The Today Show*, pp. 63–64.
7. Ibid., p. 64.
8. Walters, *Audition*, p. 171.

CHAPTER 7

1. Walters, *Audition*, p. 281.
2. Ibid., p. 287.
3. Remstein, *Barbara Walters*, p. 66.
4. Ibid.
5. Walters, *Audition*, p. 291.
6. Ibid., pp. 291–292.
7. Ibid., p. 288.
8. Ibid.
9. *Saturday Night Live* Transcripts. "Season 2, Episode 3: Baba Wawa." http://snltranscripts.jt.org/76/76cbabawawa.phtml.
10. Walters, *Audition*, p. 301.
11. Ibid., p. 303.

12. Remstein, *Barbara Walters*, p. 71.
13. Ibid., p. 69.

CHAPTER 8

1. Walters, *Audition*, p. 314.
2. Ibid., p. 315.
3. Remstein, *Barbara Walters*, p. 73.
4. Walters, *Audition*, p. 316.
5. Ibid., p. 318.
6. Ibid.
7. Ibid., p. 319.
8. Remstein, *Barbara Walters*, p. 74.
9. Walters, *Audition*, p. 323.
10. Ibid., p. 294.
11. Ibid., p. 326.
12. Ibid., p. 330.
13. Ibid.
14. Ibid., p. 338.
15. Ibid., p. 339.
16. Ibid., p. 340.
17. Ibid., p. 341.

CHAPTER 9

1. Walters, *Audition*, p. 361.
2. Remstein, *Barbara Walters*, p. 78.
3. Ibid.
4. Ibid., p. 82.
5. Walters, *Audition*, p. 425.
6. Ibid., p. 370.
7. Ibid., p. 450.
8. Ibid., p. 451.
9. Ibid., p. 531.
10. Ibid., p. 533.

CHAPTER 10

1. Remstein, *Barbara Walters*, p. 95.
2. Walters, *Audition*, p. 540.
3. Ibid., p. 541.
4. Remstein, *Barbara Walters*, p. 98.
5. Walters, *Audition*, p. 559.
6. Ibid., p. 572.
7. *The View*, ABC, September 22, 2009.

"Barbara Walters on the Record,'" Interview by Greta Van Susteren, Fox News, May 7, 2009. Available online. URL: http://www.foxnews.com/story/0,2933,519097,00. html.

Davis, Gerry. *The Today Show: An Anecdotal History*. New York: Quill William Morrow, 1987.

Deggans, Eric. "Barbara Walters: Why She's the Most Influential TV Journalist of the Modern Age," Tampabay.com, May 25, 2008. Available online. URL: http:// blogs.tampabay.com/media/2008/05/barbara-walters. html.

Dowd, Maureen. "And Now Back to You, Barbara," *New York Times*, March 25, 1990. Available online. URL: http://www.nytimes.com/1990/03/25/books/and-now-back-to-you-barbara.html.

Lemann, Nicholas. "I Have to Ask: How Barbara Walters Got Where She Is," *New Yorker*, May 12, 2008. Available online. URL: http://www.newyorker.com/arts/critics/ books/2008/05/12/080512crbo_books_lemann.

Malone, Mary. *Barbara Walters: TV Superstar*. Hillside, N.J.: Enslow Publishers, 1990.

McLeland, Susan. "Barbara Walters: U.S. Broadcast Journalist," The Museum of Broadcast Communications. Available online. URL: http://www.museum.tv/archives/ etv/W/htmlW/waltersbarb/waltersbarb.htm.

Miller, Mark Crispin. "Barbara Walters's Theater of Revenge," *Harper's*, November 1989. Available online. URL: http://www.harpers.org/archive/1989/11/0059088.

Oppenheimer, Jerry. *Barbara Walters: An Unauthorized Biography*. New York: St. Martin's Press, 1990.

Quinn, Sally. "Television Personality Looks Anew at Religion." *Washington Post*, December 21, 2006. Available

online. URL: http://newsweek.washingtonpost.com/
onfaith/guestvoices/2006/12/television_personality_
looks_a.html.

Remstein, Henna. *Barbara Walters*. Philadelphia: Chelsea
House Publishers, 1999.

Saturday Night Live Transcripts. "Season 2, Episode
3: Baba Wawa." Available online. URL: http://
snltranscripts.jt.org/76/76cbabawawa.phtml.

Walters, Barbara. *How to Talk with Practically Anybody
About Practically Anything*. New York: Dell, 1970.

———. "Lessons from the Front Lines." *Newsweek*,
October 4, 2008. Available online. URL: http://www.
newsweek.com/id/162357.

———. *Audition: A Memoir*. New York: Vintage Books,
2009.

Weich, Dave. "Barbara Walters Special." Powells.com,
May 3, 2008. Available online. URL: http://www.
powells.com/authors/barbarawalters.html.

Wiegand, David. "This Time, It's Barbara Walters' Turn
to Speak." *San Francisco Chronicle*, May 6, 2008. Available
online. URL: http://sfchronicle.us/cgi-bin/article.cgi?f=/
c/a/2008/05/06/DDTU10H1P9.DTL.

FURTHER RESOURCES

American Women in Radio & Television. *Making Waves: 50 Greatest Women in Radio and Television.* Andrews McMeel Publishing, 2001.

Collins, Gail. *When Everything Changed: The Amazing Journey of American Women from 1960 to the Present.* New York: Little, Brown and Company, 2009.

Mink, Eric, Laurie Dolphin, and Christian Brown. *This Is TODAY: A Window on Our Times.* Andrews McMeel Publishing, 2003.

Sanders, Marlene, and Marcia Rock. *Waiting for Prime Time: The Women of Television News.* Urbana: University of Illinois Press, 2004.

INDEX

PICTURE CREDITS

ABOUT THE AUTHOR

DENNIS ABRAMS is the author of several books for Chelsea House, including biographies of Barbara Park, Hamid Karzai, Albert Pujols, Xerxes, Rachael Ray, and Hillary Rodham Clinton. He attended Antioch College, where he majored in English and communications. A voracious reader since the age of three, Dennis lives in Houston, Texas, with his partner of 21 years, along with their two cats and their dog, Junie B.

LAKE OSWEGO JR. HIGH SCHOOL
2500 SW COUNTRY CLUB RD
LAKE OSWEGO, OR 97034
503-534-2335